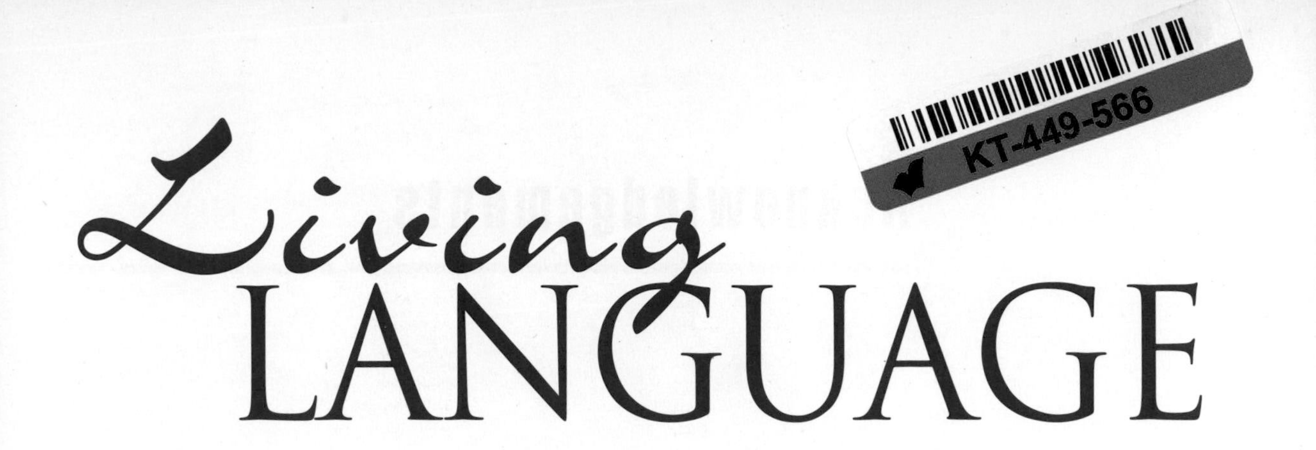


LANGUAGE AND LITERATURE

**George Keith**

Hodder & Stoughton

A MEMBER OF THE HODDER HEADLINE GROUP

# Acknowledgements

**Copyright Text:**
'beware: do not read this poem', © Ishmael Reed; 'Canons to the left' by Deborah Wolfson, © *The Guardian*, 1993; *Diamonds are Forever* by Ian Fleming © Gildrose Productions Ltd, 1956; *Educating Rita* by Willy Russell, © Casarotto Ramsey Ltd; *For Your Eyes Only* by Ian Fleming © Gildrose Productions Ltd, 1960; *From Russia with Love* by Ian Fleming © Gildrose Productions Ltd, 1957; 'l(a' is reprinted from *Complete Poems 1904–1962* by E. E. Cummings, edited by George J. Firmage, by permission of W. W. Norton & Company, © 1991 by the Trustees for the E. E. Cummings Trust and George James Firmage; 'London Airport', © Christopher Logue; 'love is more thicker than forget' is reprinted from *Complete Poems 1904–1962* by E. E. Cummings, edited by George J. Firmage, by permission of W. W. Norton & Company, © 1991 by the Trustees for the E. E. Cummings Trust and George James Firmage; *Night Falls on the City* by Sarah Gainham, © William Collins & Co. Ltd, 1967; 'Repossessing the Past: the Case for an Open Literary History', © Marilyn Butler, 1987; 'Spelling', © Margaret Atwood; *The Big Sleep* by Raymond Chandler, © Ed Victor Ltd; *The Big Sleep*, screenplay © by William Faulkner, Leigh Brackett, Jules Furthman; 'The Cool Web' by Robert Graves, © A. P. Watt; 'The Day They Shot John Lennon' © James McLure; 'The Last To Go' by Harold Pinter, in *Plays Two*, Faber, 1991; *The Sheep-pig* by Dick King-Smith © Puffin, 1985; 'To Someone Who Insisted I Look Up Someone, © X. J. Kennedy.

Every effort has been made to trace copyright holders of material reproduced in this book. Any rights not acknowledged will be acknowledged in subsequent printings if notice is given to the publisher.

Orders: please contact Bookpoint Ltd, 39 Milton Park, Abingdon, Oxon OX14 4TD. Telephone: (44) 01235 400414, Fax: (44) 01235 400454. Lines are open from 9.00 – 6.00, Monday to Saturday, wtih a 24 hour message answering service. Email address: orders@bookpoint.co.uk

*British Library Cataloguing in Publication Data*
A catalogue record for this title is available from The British Library

ISBN 0 340 73081 1
First published 1999
Impression number 10 9 8 7 6 5 4 3 2 1

Year 2005 2004 2003 2002 2001 2000 1999



Cover photo from The Ronald Grant Archive
Typeset by Fakenham Photosetting Limited, Fakenham, Norfolk NR21 8NL
Printed in Great Britain for Hodder & Stoughton Educational, a division of Hodder Headline Plc, 338 Euston Road, London NW1 3BH by Scotprint Ltd, Musselburgh, Scotland.

# Contents

# The Purpose of this Book

The chief purpose of this book is to guide A-Level students in more searching investigations of literary texts. Traditional classifications – prose fiction, poetry and drama – have been observed throughout the book, since it is texts from these principal genres of English literature that are chosen for analysis in the 'unseen' or stylistics sections of A/AS Level examination papers.

The book begins with some exploratory readings of texts in order to show how a reader's intuitive responses to their content can work effectively, and even better, when informed by critical appreciation of the language used. Analysis is not a destructive process; it will enhance both understanding and enjoyment if given the chance.

By their very nature, 'unseen' texts, whether in English Language or English Literature examinations, are intimidating. Many students suspect hidden meanings and doubt their ability to find them. Equally, many exam candidates spend a good deal of time paraphrasing the text without ever going even slightly below the surface. The suspicion is unfounded; examiners today choose passages that are likely to evoke responses and they are looking for candidates' ability to describe and explain meanings that can be constructed in the passage. Paraphrasing is largely pointless; it is perfectly understandable that you will rephrase the literal meanings of the text inside your own head just to make sure you understand them but time spent writing these down is time wasted.

Unseen texts are there to test your critical responses and to test your ability to write about them in an informed way. 'Informed' means knowing something about how language does what it does in texts, how writers write and how readers read. Social and cultural contexts also play a part. You are the prime reader so far as the examination is concerned, and you are also the prime writer. An important assessment objective in modern examinations, however, is the ability to recognise and discuss other readings. Indeed, you may yourself have more than one way of interpreting any single text. One way of defining 'different readings' is to see them as different points of view from which a text may be approached.

Being able to handle all these elements of stylistics – writer, text, reader, context – is not an easy kind of writing. It is often made up of bitty observations because much of the time you are reporting investigations into the text. The key element of course is the language itself; lose sight of that and you lose sight of the marks an examiner can give you. But the aim of writing about the bits of language is to describe and explain their effects and consequences in relation to readers' responses, contextual influences and writers' purposes. Where literary texts are concerned, 'writers' purposes' does not just mean saying meaningful things about life, love and the world in general (the message), but also practical matters such as *how* to describe events in a narrative, *what kind* of scene setting, getting the rhythm of a verse just right, or finding a way of enabling two characters to come face-to-face in Act Two, Scene Three in a way that is dramatically convincing in both action and speech.

The second chapter looks more closely at the linguistic resources available to novelists, poets and dramatists and identifies some concepts and methods that are useful for stylistic analysis. It introduces the term 'verbal art' to distinguish a vital characteristic of imaginative writing. The distinction between English literature and English language has existed for a long time but it is oddly illogical. Storytelling, poetry and scripted dialogue are all functions and forms of language so that whatever English literature does and is has to be discussed under the general concept of language. The word 'literature' technically (and after a long tradition) refers to anything that has been put into writing, whatever it is. The term 'verbal art' avoids these inconsistencies by focusing specifically on distinguishing features of language use in narratives, poems and scripts. The term also may be applied to jokes, clever advertisements, slogans and to many everyday uses of language unlikely to achieve the cultural prestige of 'literary masterpieces'.

The central chapters of the book concentrate in turn on prose fiction, poetry and drama, exploring a variety of texts in these genres. The prose fiction and drama excerpts tend to be longer than those set in examinations to give more scope for recognising issues and practising methods. Examination pieces should in time appear less formidable.

The final section demonstrates how stylistics whether applied to verbal art or any other kinds of text is in effect a multi-persective look at texts, drawing upon all areas of knowledge that make up an A-Level English language syllabus.

# 1 Back to the Classics

## Survey

In this Chapter you will be introduced to stylistic features of the three principal genres of English literature: prose fiction, poetry and drama. The texts you will investigate are:

- excerpts from *Our Mutual Friend* by Charles Dickens
- excerpts from *Tess of the D'Urbervilles* by Thomas Hardy
- poems by Donne, Wordsworth and Shelley
- a scene from *Romeo and Juliet* by William Shakespeare
- a scene from *The Importance of Being Earnest* by Oscar Wilde.

## TV Classic Serials

Readers first encountered Dickens' novel, *Our Mutual Friend*, in 19 episodes when it was published in serial form between May 1864 and November 1865 in a monthly magazine. Hardy's *Tess of the D'Urbervilles* (published in book form in 1891) was also serialised though the circumstances of its publication and reception were very different. Because the publishers feared that sexual elements in the novel would offend the taste and morals of the day, the serialised version was published in 'bowdlerised' form. (Dr Thomas Bowdler (1754–1825) became famous for his expurgated editions of Shakespeare's plays in which 'the naughty bits' had been removed, hence the verb derived from his name).

One week in March, 1998, the two novels made a second appearance in serial form, this time adapted for a medium light years away from the literary world shared by Dickens, Hardy and their readers, namely television. *Our Mutual Friend* was shown in four episodes, each repeated by BBC2; *Tess*, in two episodes on ITV. All episodes were at least one and a half hours long and viewing figures were very good.

The *Radio Times* for that week contained a feature article on the two new productions, headed:

**Television goes back to the classics this week with adaptations of two great Victorian love stories**

Notice four trigger words in this statement:

- 'classic' – quality products
- 'great' – predictable cultural evaluation
- 'Victorian' – nostalgic period pieces
- 'love stories' – universally popular theme for any tale.

Both productions were in fact excellent adaptations: moving, sensitive, powerful and completely justified in their own right. They were a legitimate, artistically satisfying 'reading' of two novels written well over a hundred years ago. Part of the success of the adaptations lies in an enduring human interest in matters of the heart and the forces of destiny. A large part of the success, however, was due to the qualities of language and imagination in the original writing.

The chapter you are now reading, as are all the following chapters, is concerned primarily with the language and imagination in original texts. This does not mean that you have to be a Victorian or a literary historian. Reading literature from any earlier period is not necessarily historical; the language is still alive whenever there is a reader to activate it, but the meanings generated may differ considerably over the years. Modern readings have value in their own right but equally important are the interpretations that a modern reader, or TV viewer, can share with a nineteenth century reader who had to wait month by month for each successive new chapter or episode to appear. What students of English Literature and of English Language have in common is the potential to read novels, poems and plays in a variety of ways and from a range of perspectives. This potential can be most fully realised by close attention to the language and by imaginative response to the text as a whole. By these means there is more pleasure to be gained from literary texts as well as more understanding.

In this chapter you will be introduced via three sets of texts, to ways of investigating the linguistic and imaginative content of literary writing. Chapter Two will then consider in more detail just what is meant by such terms as 'literature' and 'literary'.

## *Our Mutual Friend by Charles Dickens*

### ACTIVITY 1

The following excerpt is taken from *Our Mutual Friend.* The story of the whole novel consists of a complex weaving of sub-plots and parallel themes. In it there are serious villains for whom the reader may come to feel a dreadful pity in the end. Other, comic, villains also make their appearances.

The excerpt is taken from Chapter One of Book One. Young Charley Hexam is the son of a disreputable Thames boatman who scavenges for anything he can find, including dead bodies. Bradley Headstone also originates from poor circumstances but has become a school teacher with a school of his own. He has taken the ambitious Charley under his wing and in due course meets and falls in love with Charley's sister.

Read the excerpt paying particular attention to the following:

1 Listen to the dialogue in your own head. Say it to yourself fairly slowly. Savour it; imagine what sort of voice you would expect from good actors.
2 Listen also to the voice of the narrator. Imagine how Dickens might have read these parts aloud to an audience. Note where you think emphasis would be placed. Note also the shape and rhythm of the narrative sentences.
3 How 'natural' do you find the dialogue, and how much stage managed for theatrical effect? (Dickens was famous for his public readings.) Cite two or three examples. Reading them aloud to a partner will help you hear the effects much better.
4 Look in the narrative sections for examples of contrast, repetition, parenthesis (bits inserted between commas), listing of nouns and pairing or tripling of adjectives.
5 Identify two or three phrases that give you some impression of the characters of Charley Hexam and Bradley Headstone.
6 Identify words and phrases that confirm for you that the language used has the nuances of 1864 and not the late 1990s. But also keep an eye open for anything that sounds something like modern writing.
7 Sample different sentences in the narrative sections and notice any interesting structural features. For example, do any sentences begin with 'and'? If so, why do you think they are there?
8 Do you detect a semantic field in the text? Do not read the commentary until you have completed the above activities.

Even in this temple of good intentions, an exceptionally sharp boy exceptionally determined to learn, could learn something, and, having learned it, could impart it much better than the teachers; as being more knowing than they, and not at the disadvantage in which they stood towards the shrewder pupils. In this way it had come about that Charley Hexam had risen in the jumble, taught in the jumble, and been received from the jumble into a better school.

'So you want to go and see your sister, Hexam?'

'If you please, Mr. Headstone.'

'I have half a mind to go with you. Where does your sister live?'

'Why, she is not settled yet, Mr. Headstone. I'd rather you didn't see her till she's settled, if it was all the same to you.'

'Look here, Hexam.' Mr. Bradley Headstone, highly certificated stipendiary schoolmaster, drew his right forefinger through one of the buttonholes of the boy's coat, and looked at it attentively. 'I hope your sister may be good company for you?'

'Why do you doubt it, Mr. Headstone?'

'I did not say I doubted it.'

'No sir; you didn't say so.'

Bradley Headstone looked at his finger again, took it out of the buttonhole and looked at it closer, bit the side of it and looked at it again.

'You see, Hexam, you will be one of us. In good time you are sure to pass a creditable examination and become one of us. Then the question is –'

The boy waited so long for the question, while the schoolmaster looked at a new side of his finger, and bit it, and looked at it again, that at length the boy repeated:

'The question is, sir –?'

'Whether you had not better leave well alone.'

'Is it well to leave my sister alone, Mr. Headstone?'

'I do not say so, because I do not know. I put it to you, I ask you to think of it. I want you to consider. You know how well you are doing here.'

'After all, she got me here,' said the boy with a struggle.

'Perceiving the necessity of it,' acquiesced the schoolmaster, 'and making up her mind fully to the separation. Yes.'

The boy, with a return of that former reluctance or struggle or whatever it was, seemed to debate with himself. At length he said, raising his eyes to the master's face:

'I wish you'd come with me and see her, Mr. Headstone, though she is not settled. I wish you'd come with me, and take her in the rough, and judge for yourself.'

'You are sure you would not like,' asked the schoolmaster, 'to prepare her?'

'My sister Lizzie,' said the boy, proudly, 'wants no preparing, Mr. Headstone. What she is, she is, and shows herself to be. There's no pretending about my sister.'

His confidence in her sat more easily upon him than the indecision with which he had twice contended. It was his better nature to be true to her, if it were his worse nature to be wholly selfish. And as yet the better nature had the stronger hold.

'Well, I can spare the evening,' said the schoolmaster. 'I am ready to walk with you.'

'Thank you, Mr. Headstone. And I am ready to go.'

Bradley Headstone, in his decent black coat and waistcoat, and decent white shirt, and decent black formal tie, and decent pantaloons of pepper and salt, with his decent silver watch in his pocket and its decent hair-guard round his neck, looked a thoroughly decent young man of six-and-twenty. He was never seen in any other dress, and yet there was a certain stiffness in his manner of wearing this, as if there were a want of adaptation between him and it, recalling some mechanics in their holiday clothes. He had acquired mechanically a great store of teacher's knowledge. He could do mental arithmetic mechanically, sing at sight mechanicaly, blow various wind instruments mechanically, even play the great church organ mechanically. From his early childhood up, his mind had been a place of mechancial stowage. The arrangement of his wholesale warehouse, so that it might be always ready to meet the demands of retail dealers – history here, geography there, astronomy to the right, political economy to the left – natural history, the physical sciences, figures, music, the lower mathematics, and what not, all in their places – this care had imparted to his countenance a look of care; while the habit of questioning and being questioned had given him a suspicious manner, or a manner that would be better described as one of lying in wait. There was a kind of settled trouble in the face. It was the face belonging to a naturally slow or inattentive intellect that had toiled hard to get what it had won, and that had to hold it now that it was gotten. He always seemed to be uneasy lest anything should be missing from his mental warehouse, and taking stock to assure himself.

Suppression of so much to make room for so much, had given him a constrained manner, over and above. Yet there was enough of what was animal, and of what was fiery (though smouldering), still visible in him, to suggest that if young Bradley Headstone, when a pauper lad, had chanced to be told off for the sea, he would not have been the last man in a ship's crew. Regarding that origin of his, he was proud, moody, and sullen, desiring it to be forgotten. And few people knew of it.

In some visits to the jumble his attention had been drawn to this boy Hexam. An undeniable boy for a pupil-teacher; an undeniable boy to do credit to the master who should bring him on. Combined with this consideration there may have been some thought of the pauper lad now never to be mentioned. Be that how it might, he had with pains gradually worked the boy into his own school, and procured him some offices to discharge there, which were repaid with food and lodging. Such were the circumstances that had brought together Bradley Headstone and young Charley Hexam that autumn evening.

## COMMENTARY

1 The text is an excerpt from a whole novel but nevertheless the dialogue is set within a narrative context supplied in the first nine lines which describe Charley. Headstone's first remark is terse and ends with a formal, surname address. There is a variety of respect signals in Charley's speech: 'Mr', 'if you please', 'if it was all the same to you'.

There are interesting pragmatic features too, which a reading aloud with a partner should reveal. There is an element of insinuation and implied meaning in what Headstone goes on to say. Charley appears to pick up an implied meaning that is immediately contradicted:

'Why do you doubt it . . . ?'
'I did not say I doubted it.'

Headstone's speech is accompanied by neurotic, maybe slightly menacing actions, for example, the finger in the button hole and the biting. The delay following 'Then the question is . . .' is not unlike the modern theatrical technique of Harold Pinter in which pauses have as much power and meaning as words. Notice the pause neatly inserted by the narrative voice interrupting Headstone's voice in:

'You are sure you would not like', asked the schoolmaster, 'to prepare her?'

This reflects the art of a compellingly theatrical storyteller and is reinforced by the instinctive rounding off of the conversation:

'Thank you Mr Headstone. And I am ready to go'.

Throughout there is a guardedness in the conversation which the reader hears. It echoes real life experience but is written with theatrical emphasis. Psychologically, the exchange is finely balanced between an intensely neurotic teacher and a cautious, yet quick witted pupil on the make.

**2** A quite long first sentence conveys the basic rhythm of Dickens' prose. There's a combination of exactness and emphasis. Notice the effect of the semi-colon, signalling a pause in the flow of thought. There are six commas in the first sentence, in addition to the semi-colon, and two in the second. Take note of these in a reading aloud because they indicate the way the narrator thinks; they are not pauses for breath, though they do come at the right place for taking a breath.

The latter part of the excerpt is entirely narrative devoted to comment on the life and character of Headstone. It concludes by drawing together the lives of Charley and Headstone. There is a slight but detectable air of foreboding in the narrative voice: 'He always seemed to be uneasy . . .', 'And few people knew of it,' '. . . one lying in wait', and the final sentence of the excerpt.

Notice how there is an alternation of very long and quite short sentences which punctuate paragraphs, not with punctuation marks on the page, but with pauses in the flow of ideas. Look, for example, at the paragraph beginning: 'Bradley Headstone, in his decent black coat . . .' down to '. . . to assure himself'. Observe the placing of the following:

**a** 'He had acquired mechanically a great store of teacher's knowledge'.
**b** 'There was a kind of settled trouble in his face'.

There are ten words in each, though this may just be coincidental.

Much of the dramatic and theatrical effect in Dickens' writing is achieved by the pauses that precede and follow short sentences. Part of reading the text is hearing these effects in the mind's ear, as though you were being read to. Do not reject the idea of being read to, as though it is something you have grown out of. Critical appreciation of the stylistic features of literary texts depends as much on a listening ear that hears sounds and voices as on a seeing eye that visualises text.

**3** The context in which Hexam and Headstone are talking is a naturalistic one, and there are a number of words and phrases characteristic of everyday conversation:

- beginning an utterance with 'so' as in the first remark
- elisions as in 'she's' and 'didn't'
- 'half a mind'
- second person pronoun as in 'You see, Hexam . . .'

- uncompleted utterances as in 'the question is . . .'
- using a phrase such as 'After all . . .'.

The actual content of the dialogue takes place in real time (in the time it takes to say it), but the narrator sometimes interrupts the flow of real time with some comment or effect. There are quite long interruptions, for example, between:

'Look here, Hexam . . .' / 'I hope your sister . . .' and 'Theres no pretending about my sister' / '. . . walk with you'.

Elsewhere, Dickens comments on the time factor: 'The boy waited so long for the question . . .' and 'At length he said . . .'.

The dialogue may seem natural enough, with a few period features in the language and a certain theatricality in Dickens' writing. The speakers do have individual identities and are depicted interacting, that is speaking and listening to each other. It is important, however, not to be deluded by these appearances into thinking that the speech and the characters are 'real'. This may seem a rather obvious thing to say but the language of fiction has enormous imaginative power. Television companies regularly receive heartfelt letters whose writers seem to believe in the real existence of soap opera characters. Often people do not know the name of the actor, only the name of the character. In English Literature examinations also, it is not unusual to find candidates writing about characters in fiction as though they had an identity of their own. In fact, everything – dialogue, character, situation, plot – is constructed inside the author's head.

The dialogue of characters has to be 'heard' in the context of the narrator's own voice, ever present but never, in good writing, intrusive. The pause during the question for example could well occur in a real, everyday conversation, but Dickens here gets the timimg just right for theatrical effect (as in a public reading for entertainment) in a way that is rarely achieved in real life. The neatly echoing finale to the conversation has already been noted:

'I am ready to walk with you'.
'I am ready to go'.

**4** Throughout the excerpt there are instances in which Dickens uses, consciously or subconsciously, language tricks or strategies for particular effects:

**repetitions**: jumble, I (in 'I do not say'), nature, decent, mechanically, so much, undeniable.

**lexico-grammatical patterns**: 'risen in the . . . taught in the . . . and been received' (note the twist in the last one); the three references to Headstone's finger (plus two to the buttonhole); 'of what was animal, and of what was fiery'.

**modifying sequences**: 'highly certificated stipendiary'; 'naturally slow or inattentive'; 'proud, moody and sullen'.

**parenthesis**: '(though smouldering)'; '– history here . . . several places –'; and the long insertion between 'Bradley Headstone . . .' and the main verb phrase at the end of the paragraph concerned, '... looked a thoroughly decent young man.'

**5** Language in texts works by both explicit description and statement and by implicit means. Implied meanings in texts need not be mysterious if you develop a knack for noticing them. In everyday life everybody notices implied meanings. When somebody asks a question 'Do you always behave like this?' we detect an implied critical statement. Similarly the statement 'It is hot in here' can imply a polite command, 'somebody open one of the windows'. Character is frequently conveyed by the explicit and the implicit.

At the beginning of the excerpt Dickens makes a number of explicit remarks about Charley Hexam that convey impressions of character – the whole of the first paragraph in fact. Notice too how the phrases 'an exceptionally sharp boy' and 'exceptionally determined' are echoed in the final paragraph by the repeated phrase, 'an undeniable boy'.

If you allow yourself to step back a little from the actual conversation between Hexam and Headstone you could notice how shrewdly and confidently Charley takes his part in it which raises a question of whether the two are equally matched or whether one is dominant. These are matters which Dickens leaves the reader to infer.

There are many explicit comments by Dickens on the character of Headstone. They are almost overbearing for example the long paragraph beginning: 'Bradley Headstone in his decent black coat ...'.

The remark, 'highly certificated stipendiary schoolmaster' works both explicitly and implicitly. It supplies a biographical detail, an item of curriculum vitae if you like, but there is also the implication that that is how Headstone sees himself. Sometimes implicit character drawing is achieved by discussing explicitly a specific action. Some readers may detect a manic quality in the way that Mr Headstone bites the side of his finger.

**6** The mode of address, 'sir', hints at an earlier period, confirmed by such phrases as 'if you please', 'wants no preparing', 'it was gotten' and 'lest anything should be missing'. Modern readers may feel that the talk has a characteristic literary formality about it, and wonder if people really talked like this.

7 The narrative paragraphs are launched in different ways:

- 'Even in this temple ...'
- 'Bradley Headstone ...'
- 'Suppression of so much ...'
- 'In some visits ...'

Dickens' concern in these longer paragraphs is to construct characters and situations by drawing immediate sketches of character and by supplying appropriate fictional information, for example, of Headstone's origins. He does this with a supremely confident storytelling manner and with a delight in verbal performance. This conscious shaping of expression through lexical choice and sentence construction is characteristic of verbal art, and it will recur throughout the examples you will be investigating.

Hexam's final remark begins with an 'And . . .', something you might expect in literary dialogue reflecting natural speech. The conjunction 'and' is very frequently used in this way. It follows a pause yet keeps a continuity going; more especially here, it conveys an emphasis to the beginning of a remark that rounds off the scene. Dickens also uses 'and' to begin sentences that round off narrative paragraphs:

'And as yet the better nature had the stronger hold'
'And few people knew of it'.

The view that 'and' should not be used to begin written sentences is well known. Generally speaking, the view is a sensible one, especially when guiding inexperienced writers away from the patterns and norms of speech into the conventions of the written word. If a writer uses 'and' in this way frequently and without thought, it is a sign of lack of control over the writing; there is no need to prohibit it, however, on some grammatical ground. To argue, for example, that the word is a conjunction, which in the initial position of a sentence, isn't in fact joining anything, is no longer convincing. Other conjunctions are frequently used in both initial and 'middle' sentence positions: 'if', 'because', 'when'. It is a matter of style.

Dickens ends two narrative paragraphs in this excerpt with sentences beginning with 'and', in extremely effective ways. One is fairly short in length, the other very short. Both achieve the rhetorical effect of rounding off the paragraph in a dramatic or 'clinching' way. The emphasis is unmistakable, while the use of 'and' keeps the final remark in contact with what has gone before. There is a logic to its use but these two examples show how 'strict' grammar hands over to rhetoric to permit even more effective communication. It is also a concise strategy. Note, incidentally, in the first paragraph, how Dickens is extremely punctilious in making the initial, long sentence grammatically tidy. Look at the five internal punctuation marks.

It is likely that written sentences beginning with 'and' will not only be infrequent, but also short. Notice too, how 'and' was used at the end of a sentence for a particular dramatic effect; as a one word utterance in conversation it signifys an implied question, making a bridge to the answer.

A little issue such as this draws attention to differences and connections between speech and writing. Another similar issue is whether or when you can use elisions, like 'can't'. Novelists and poets, for example, take care, either by instinct, conscious effort, or both, to judge carefully the language they use. At the same time they show concern for the 'voice' that is coming across. The problem for both experienced, talented writers and A-Level students is striking a balance between following formal writing conventions and expressing a personal voice that will be closer to speech – but not too close.

**8** There is quite clearly a semantic field of education underlying the excerpt, and within that, another field to do with mechanisms and arithmetic, reinforcing the 'mental warehouse' and taking stock metaphors. Frequent abstract noun phrases such as 'temple of good intentions', 'a return to that former reluctance', 'the indecision', 'better nature', 'worse nature', 'the circumstances' are all given flesh by the use elsewhere by the imaginative selection of vivid detail and the use of metaphor.

## ACTIVITY 2

Look at the excerpt below, also from *Our Mutual Friend.* It describes a meeting between two other characters in the book, Silas Wegg, a one-legged rascal with a smattering of education, and Mr Venus, a taxidermist and a preparer of anatomical specimens for medical study. Wegg has previously had an accident in which he lost a leg. The leg was subsequently sold by a hospital porter to Mr Venus. If you find the story so far, grotesquely comic, read on for further revelations. Silas Wegg has visited Mr Venus in the hope of getting his leg back.

Read the excerpt two or three times, giving consideration to the points listed below. Remember, read slowly (preferably aloud), listening to the pauses, the insinuations, the emphasis, the different voices and the interplay. Relish words or ideas that are particularly macabre or juicy.

Mr. Wegg, as an artful man who is sure of his supper by-and-by, presses muffin on his host to soothe him into a compliant state of mind, or, as one might say, to grease his works. As the muffins disappear, little by little, the black shelves and nooks and corners begin to appear, and Mr. Wegg gradually acquires an imperfect notion that over against him on the chimney-piece is a Hindoo baby in a bottle, curved up with his big head tucked under him, as though he would instantly throw a summersault if the bottle were large enough.

When he deems Mr. Venus's wheels sufficiently lubricated, Mr. Wegg approaches his object by asking, as he lightly taps his hands together, to express an undesigning frame of mind:

'And how have I been going on, this long time, Mr. Venus?'

'Very bad,' says Mr. Venus, uncompromisingly.

'What? Am I still at home?' asks Mr. Wegg, with an air of surprise.

'Always at home.'

This would seem to be secretly agreeable to Wegg, but he veils his feelings, and observes, 'Strange. To what do you attribute it?'

'I don't know,' replies Venus, who is a haggard melancholy man, speaking in a weak voice of querulous complaint, 'to what to attribute it, Mr. Wegg. I can't work you into a miscellaneous one, nohow. Do what I will, you can't be got to fit. Anybody with a passable knowledge would pick you out at a look, and say – "No go! Don't match!"'

'Well, but hang it, Mr. Venus,' Wegg expostulates with some little irritation, 'that can't be personal and peculiar in *me*. It must often happen with miscellaneous ones.'

'With ribs (I grant you) always. But not else. When I prepare a miscellaneous one, I know beforehand that I can't keep to nature, and be miscellaneous with ribs, because every man has his own ribs, and no other man's will go with them; but elseways I can be miscellaneous. I have just sent home a Beauty – a perfect Beauty – to a school of art. One leg Belgian, one leg English, and the pickings of eight other people in it. Talk of not being qualified to be miscellaneous! By rights you *ought* to be, Mr. Wegg.'

Silas looks as hard at his one leg as he can in the dim light, and after a pause sulkily opines 'that it must be the fault of the other people. Or how do you mean to say it comes about?' he demands impatiently.

'I don't know how it comes about. Stand up a minute. Hold the light.' Mr. Venus takes from a corner by his chair, the bones of a leg and foot, beautifully pure, and put together with exquisite neatness. These he compares with Mr. Wegg's leg; that gentleman looking on, as if he were being measured for a riding-boot. 'No, I don't know how it is, but so it is. You have got a twist in that bone, to the best of my belief. I *never* saw the likes of you.'

Mr. Wegg having looked distrustfully at his own limb, and suspiciously at the pattern with which it had been compared, makes the point:

'I'll bet a pound that ain't an English one!'

'An easy wager, when we run so much into foreign! No, it belongs to that French gentleman.'

As he nods towards a point of darkness behind Mr. Wegg, the latter, with a slight start, looks round for 'that French gentleman,' whom he at length decries to be represented (in a very workmanlike manner) by his ribs only, standing on a shelf in another corner, like a piece of armour or a pair of stays.

'Oh!' says Mr. Wegg, with a sort of sense of being introduced; 'I dare say you were all right enough in your own country, but I hope no objections will be taken to my saying that the Fenchman was never yet born as I should wish to match.'

At this moment the greasy door is violently pushed inward, and a boy follows it, who says, after having let it slam:

'Come for the stuffed canary.'

'It's three and ninepence,' returns Venus; 'have you got the money?'

The boy produces four shillings. Mr. Venus, always in exceedingly low spirits, and making whimpering sounds, peers about for the stuffed canary. On his taking the candle to assist his search, Mr. Wegg observes that he has a convenient little shelf near his knees, exclusively appropriate to skeleton hands, which have very much the appearance of wanting to lay hold of him. From these Mr. Venus rescues the canary in a glass case, and shows it to the boy.

'There!' he whimpers. 'There's animation! On a twig, making up his mind to hop! Take care of him; he's a lovely specimen. – And three is four.'

The boy gathers up his change and has pulled the door open by a leather strap nailed to it for the purpose, when Venus cries out:

'Stop him! Come back, you young villain! You've got a tooth among them halfpence.'

'How was I to know I'd got it? You giv it me. I don't want none of your teeth. I've got enough of my own.' So the boy pipes as he selects it from his change, and throws it on the counter.

'Don't sauce *me* in the wicious pride of your youth,' Mr. Venus retorts pathetically. 'Don't hit *me* because you see I'm down. I'm low enough without that. It dropped into the till I suppose. They drop into everything. There was two in the coffee-pot at breakfast-time. Molars.'

'Very well, then,' argues the boy, 'what do you call names for?'

To which Mr. Venus only replies, shaking his shock of dusty hair, and winking his weak eyes, 'Don't sauce *me* in the wicious pride of your youth; don't hit *me* because I'm down. You've no idea how small you'd come out, if I had the articulating of you.'

This consideration seems to have its effect upon the boy, for he goes out grumbling.

'Oh dear me, dear me!' sighs Mr. Venus, heavily, snuffing the candle, 'the world that appeared so flowery has ceased to blow! You're casting your eye round the shop, Mr. Wegg. Let me show you a light. My working bench. My young man's bench. A Wice. Tools. Bones, warious. Preserved Indian baby. African ditto. Bottled preparations, warious. Everything within reach of your hand, in good preservation. The mouldy ones a-top. What's in those hampers over them again, I don't quite remember. Say, human, warious. Cats. Articulated English baby. Dogs. Ducks. Glass eyes, warious. Mummied bird. Dried cuticle, warious. Oh dear me! That's the general panoramic view.'

1 What is the humour that lies behind Wegg's use of the first person 'I' in his first remark?
2 A very basic formula for writing direct speech is: 'Mr A said . . .' or '. . . said Mr A'. Look through the excerpt and list the different ways in which Dickens weaves what his characters say into the narrative as a whole. What opportunities are there here for the narrator?
3 Identify two or three examples of black comedy.
4 Identify one or two instances where Dickens trusts the reader to understand what is going on without needing to spell it out. Look, for example, at '– And three is four'.
5 Identify one or two ways in which Dickens enables the reader to 'hear' the way in which something is said.
6 Sometimes writers add very specific information about the manner in which something has been said, which usually gives a strong impression of character ('impatiently' or 'with some little irritation'). List occasions when Dickens does this and describe the effect on you the reader.
7 What semantic field is created in the excerpt? Identify any words that seem especially striking, for example, 'articulator'.
8 Finally, as an exercise in style, you could write an alternative section in Dickens' narrative. The introduction of a youth buying a canary is a diversion which adds to the atmosphere of the scene but is irrelevant to the plot. To get under the skin of Dickens' style, delete from the excerpt the section beginning, 'and a boy follows it' to '. . . goes out grumbling'. Substitute a passage about a customer of your own invention, but written in a style and imagination that blends with that of Dickens. Make it about the same length as the deleted section. The customer could be a sailor collecting a stuffed parrot, a poor medical student wishing to purchase a skull or a woman with an ancient, mummified cat to sell. Make up your own!

Note that the second excerpt is written in the present tense, while the first one is written in the past tense. Make sure your own writing is in the present. Why do you think there should be this variation? You could look at a copy of the novel in the library and investigate which tense is used at the beginning of each chapter.

**ACTIVITY 3**

Compare the ways in which the Headstone/Hexam and the Wegg/Venus conversations are constructed. Do you detect common elements that add up to a particular style or technique? Look especially at the way in which the narrator intervenes.

## *Tess of the D'Urbervilles by Thomas Hardy*

You are now going to look at two excerpts from Thomas Hardy's *Tess of the D'Urbervilles.*

**ACTIVITY 4**

In the first extract below, Tess is working in the fields at harvest time. Seduced by her employer and supposed benefactor, Tess now has a child to feed and care for. The excerpt is the opening part of Chapter Fourteen. It consists of continuous narrative with no conversation. Read it through at least twice, savouring the sights, sounds and other impressions created by the writer.

It was a hazy sunrise in August. The denser nocturnal vapours, attacked by the warm beams, were dividing and shrinking into isolated fleeces within hollows and coverts, where they waited till they should be dried away to nothing.

The sun, on account of the mist, had a curious sentient, personal look, demanding the masculine pronoun for its adequate expression. His present aspect, coupled with the lack of all human forms in the scene, explained the old-time heliolatries in a moment. One could feel that a saner religion had never prevailed under the sky. The luminary was a golden-haired beaming, mild-eyed, God-like creature, gazing down in the vigour and intentness of youth upon an earth that was brimming with interest for him.

His light, a little later, broke through chinks of cottage shutters, throwing stripes like red-hot pokers upon cupboards, chests of drawers, and other furniture within; and awakening harvesters who were not already astir.

But of all ruddy things that morning the brightest were two broad arms of painted wood, which rose from the margin of a yellow cornfield hard by Marlott village. They, with two others below, formed the revolving Maltese cross of the reaping-machine, which had been brought to the field on the previous evening to be ready for operations this day. The paint with which they were smeared, intensified in hue by the sunlight, imparted to them a look of having been dipped in liquid fire.

The field had already been 'opened'; that is to say, a lane a few feet wide had been hand-cut through the wheat along the whole circumference of the field, for the first passage of the horses and machine.

Two groups, one of men and lads, the other of women, had come down the lane just at the hour when the shadows of the eastern hedge-top struck the west hedge midway, so that the heads of the groups were enjoying sunrise while their feet were still in the dawn. They disappeared from the lane between the two stone posts which flanked the nearest field-gate.

Presently there arose from within a ticking like the love-making of the grasshopper. The machine had begun, and a moving concatenation of three horses and the aforesaid long rickety machine was visible over the gate, a driver sitting upon one of the hauling horses, and an attendant on the seat of the implement. Along one side of the field the whole wain went, the arms of the mechanical reaper revolving slowly, till it passed down the hill quite out of sight. In a minute it came up on the other side of the field at the same equable pace; the glistening brass star in the forehead of the fore horse first catching the eye as it rose into view over the stubble, then the bright arms, and then the whole machine.

The narrow lane of stubble encompassing the field grew wider with each circuit, and the standing corn was reduced to smaller area as the morning wore on. Rabbits, hares, snakes, rats, mice, retreated inwards as into a fastness, unaware of the ephemeral nature of their refuge, and of the doom that awaited them later in the day when, their covert shrinking to a more and more horrible narrowness, they were huddled together, friends and foes, till the last few yards of upright wheat fell also under the teeth of the unerring reaper, and they were every one put to death by the sticks and stones of the harvesters.

The reaping-machine left the fallen corn behind it in little heaps, each heap being of the quantity for a sheaf; and upon these the active binders in the rear laid their hands – mainly women, but some of them men in print shirts, and trousers supported round their waists by leather straps, rendering useless the two buttons behind, which twinkled and bristled with sunbeams at every movement of each wearer, as if they were a pair of eyes in the small of his back.

But those of the other sex were the most interesting of this company of binders, by reason of the charm which is acquired by woman when she becomes part and parcel of outdoor nature, and is not merely an object set down therein as at ordinary times. A field-man is a personality afield; a field-woman is a portion of the field; she has somehow lost her own margin, imbibed the essence of her surrounding, and assimilated herself with it.

The women – or rather girls, for they were mostly young – wore drawn cotton bonnets with great flapping curtains to keep off the sun, and gloves to prevent their hands being wounded by the stubble. There was one wearing a pale pink jacket, another in a cream-coloured tight-sleeved gown, another in a petticoat as red as the arms of the reaping-machine; and others, older, in the brown-rough 'wropper' or over-all – the old-established and most appropriate dress of the field-woman, which the young ones were abandoning. This morning the eye returns involuntarily to the girl in the pink cotton jacket, she being the most flexuous and finely-drawn figure of them all. But her bonnet is pulled so far over her brow that none of her face is disclosed while she binds, though her complexion may be guessed from a stray twine or two of dark brown bair which extends below the curtain of her bonnet. Perhaps one reason why she seduces casual attention is that she never courts it, though the other women often gaze around them.

Her binding proceeds with clock-like monotony. From the sheaf last finished she draws a handful of ears, patting their tips with her left palm to bring them even. Then stooping low she moves forward, gathering the corn with both hands against her knees, and pushing her left gloved hand under the bundle to meet the right on the other side, holding the corn in an embrace like that of a lover. She brings the ends of the bond together, and kneels on the sheaf while she ties it, beating back her skirts now and then when lifted by the breeze. A bit of her naked arm is visible between the buff leather of the gauntlet and the sleeve of her gown; and as the day wears on its feminine smoothness becomes scarified by the stubble, and bleeds.

At intervals she stands up to rest, and to retie her disarranged apron, or to pull her bonnet straight. Then one can see the oval face of a handsome young woman with deep dark eyes and long heavy clinging tresses, which seem to clasp in a beseeching way anything they fall against. The cheeks are paler, the teeth more regular, the red lips thinner than is usual in a country-bred girl.

It is Tess Durbeyfield, otherwise d'Urberville, somewhat changed – the same, but not the same; at the present stage of her existence living as a stranger and an alien here, though it was no strange land that she was in. After a long seclusion she had come to a resolve to undertake outdoor work in her native village, the busiest season of the year in the agricultural world having arrived, and nothing that she could do within the house being so remunerative for the time as harvesting in the fields.

1 Look at the first ten paragraphs and note what topic change or change in point of view occurs with each paragraph. 'Point of view' can literally mean 'what is being looked at in the scene depicted' but it can also refer to what the narrator chooses to reflect upon. How does the writer guide your viewing of the scene, paragraph by paragraph?

2 It is quite unusual for a novelist to provide a linguistic commentary on his writing as Hardy does at the beginning of the second paragraph. A literary term for the point Hardy makes is 'personification'. Compare two aspects of language use in this excerpt: poetic, figurative effects such as personification, metaphor, simile; and vivid but nevertheless literal writing that would be of use to an agricultural historian, for example. Note places where poetic imagining of the scene and an eye for actual details are blended together. Look, for example at some of the adjective/noun combinations: hazy sunrise; golden-haired, beaming, mild-eyed, God-like creature; liquid fire.

3 Half way through paragraph 11, Hardy introduces the figure of Tess. Describe the

effect of Hardy's narrative technique from the first word of the excerpt up to the sentence beginning, 'This morning the eye returns involuntarily to the girl in the pink cotton jacket . . .'? What is the difference in effect between 'That morning' and 'This morning'? Whose 'eye' might 'return involuntarily'? Where does the narrator implicitly 'place' the reader in relation to the scene?

4 The word picture of Tess is vividly drawn. Make two lists: one containing relatively objective description, the other indicating words or phrases that reveal the narrator's feelings about Tess and which lead the reader to similar feelings.

5 How do you react/respond to Hardy's way here of writing about women? Before answering this, list examples. What, for example, is the semantics of: 'A field-man is a personality afield; a field-woman is a portion of the field; she has somehow lost her own margin . . .'?

6 Look at different kinds of lexis in the excerpt. Do you feel there is a contrast, for example between the groups of words and phrases in the box below:

| | |
|---|---|
| chinks; rickety; part and parcel; A bit of; old-time; 'wropper'. | the denser nocturnal vapours; a moving concatenation; flexuous and finely drawn; the ephemeral nature of their refuge. |

**COMMENTARY**

1 Four of the commonest ways to begin a chapter are:

- setting the scene
- reporting conversation or thoughts
- describing events and action
- expressing thoughts and comments directly to the reader.

Hardy goes to considerable lengths to set the scene in this excerpt together with some reflections on women, agricultural life and the story so far. Things happen in the excerpt but the main literary purpose is atmospheric scene setting. You have only to list visual references to confirm this. Starting with a 'hazy sunrise' the point of view in the text moves from the sun, looking down on the earth, to a field in which a reaping-machine is at work followed by groups of farm labourers, men and women. A group of women then becomes the focus one of whom is wearing a pale pink jacket. Finally, Hardy focuses attention on Tess. Notice how the text refers back to the woman in the pale, pink jacket, rather like a movie camera returning for a closer look.

This is in fact what we would now think of as a cinematic way of writing. In modern TV terms, for example, the authorial comment would be condensed in a voice-over narration, or the camera itself would be a silent narrator.

In order to explore in more detail the narrative technique employed here you could take a creative stylistics approach and write a few paragraphs along similar lines. Working upwards and outwards first of all, you could invent a single person engaged in an activity within a group, then set the immediate scene and finally move out to a distant vantage point, from which your written narrative would begin. You will need to select the vantage point, realistic or fanciful, and have one or two reflections of your own beyond describing what you see. The opening of Leon Garfield's novel, *Smith*, for example, is written from the point of view of birds high up among the London rooftops at night, looking down upon a mugging about to take place.

**2** The turning of the sun into a God-like person looking down on the activities of mortals registers immediately with readers.

The whole scene is packed with informative description, framed in a strong imaginative view of the countryside and its workers. There are details of the reaping-machine, the behaviour of disturbed field animals, the clothes people wear, the actions of harvesters, and the appearance of the corn. Yet there are nearly as many imaginative touches. The factual 'A stray twine or two of dark brown hair' contrasts with the imaginative 'tresses which seem to clasp in a beseeching way'.

The 'seem to' makes all the difference. Look also at 'a look of having been dipped in liquid fire' and compare it with 'A lane had been hand-cut through the wheat along the whole circumference of the field'. Compare also, a 'ticking like the love-making of the grasshopper' with 'She brings the ends of the bond together, and kneels on the sheaf while she ties it, beating back her skirts now and then when lifted by the breeze'. The reference to love-making adds a nuance to the scene but the literalness of the second quotation has its own poetic quality in the context of the scene.

**3** The demonstrative pronoun 'this' (it can also be called a 'determiner') in 'this morning' conveys a sense of immediate time and close proximity. It is involving whereas 'that' has a distancing effect. As shown earlier, Hardy's narrative technique directs the reader's inner eye from a high point in the heavens toward a close-up of Tess in a field below.

**4** Some literal descriptions of Tess have already been cited, others are: 'her bonnet pulled so far over her brow that none of her face is disclosed' and 'A bit of her naked arm is visible between the buff leather of the gauntlet and the sleeve of her gown' – all painterly details. But Hardy also writes: 'holding the corn in an embrace like that of a lover' and 'The cheeks are paler, the teeth more regular, the lips thinner . . .'. The use of 'like' immediately signals the author's imagination at work, as do the three comparatives making a qualitative judgement about the character. Describing her as a 'stranger' and an 'alien' in the last paragraph also expresses and generates feeling.

**5** There are a number of gender references in this excerpt. The sun demands 'the masculine pronoun for adequate expression' because of its 'curious sentient, personal look'. The notion of personality in relation to masculinity occurs again a little later: 'A fieldman is a personality afield; a field-woman is a portion of the field; and has somehow lost her own margin'. Woman is also described in this scene as 'part and parcel of outdoor nature . . . not merely an object set down therein'. Such a state of existence is referred to as 'the charm which is acquired by woman'. Note the generic term 'woman'.

**6** The narrative voice of this excerpt is Victorian, educated, and literary, using quite a lot of Latinate vocabulary:

concatenation, circumference, encompassing, assimilated, luminary, flexuous.

Words like 'heliolatries' (religions that worship the sun) and 'scarified' are Greek in origin.

Hardy does, however, make some explicit references to words of dialectal and/or agricultural origin: The field had already been 'opened' (note Hardy's own use of inverted commas); 'wropper'; a shock or 'stitch' as it was called; and 'Tess Durbeyfield, otherwise D'Urberville'.

## ACTIVITY 5

The following excerpt occurs later in the novel. Tess now works at the Talbothay dairy. Sadly, her child has died but she is beginning to find happiness again in her new life. She has fallen in love with a man called Angel Clare. Read the excerpt, 'listening' to the dialogue, and consider the following:

1 The second paragraph mainly describes narrative events, whereas the first and third paragraphs do something different. Describe the effects of these paragraphs on your imagination, ensuring that you identify what it is that creates those effects. Look, for example, at the verb 'slept' and the noun 'snores'. Look at the mixture of everyday observation (realistic description) and imagination (note the metaphors).
2 The sensuousness of some of Hardy's writing worried the original publishers because they feared it would shock Victorian readers. Identify some sensuous effects in the excerpt. How many physical references are there, for example?
3 How does the language of Angel Clare's proposal contrast with the language of the preceding two paragraphs?
4 The situation described is clearly an emotionally charged one. Look at the resources Hardy uses to make conversation as realistic as possible. Notice, for example, the use of punctuation.

Not a human being was out of doors at the dairy. The denizens were all enjoying the usual afternoon nap of an hour or so which the exceedingly early hours kept in the summer-time rendered a necessity. At the door the wood-hooped pails, sodden and bleached by infinite scrubbings, hung like hats on a stand upon the forked and peeled limb of an oak fixed there for that purpose; all of them ready and dry for the evening milking. Angel entered, and went through the silent passages of the house to the back quarters, where he listened for a moment. Sustained snores came from the cart-house, where some of the men were lying down; the grunt and squeal of sweltering pigs arose from the still further distance. The large-leaved rhubarb and cabbage plants slept too, their broad limp surfaces hanging in the sun like half-closed umbrellas.

He unbridled and fed his horse, and as he re-entered the house the clock struck three. Three was the afternoon skimming-hour; and, with the stroke, Clare heard the creaking of the floor-boards above, and then the touch of a descending foot on the stairs. It was Tess's, who in another moment came down before his eyes.

She had not heard him enter, and hardly realized his presence there. She was yawning, and he saw the red interior of her mouth as if it had been a snake's. She had stretched one arm so high above her coiled-up cable of hair that he could see its satin delicacy above the sunburn; her face was flushed with sleep, and her eyelids hung heavy over their pupils. The brim-fulness of her nature breathed from her. It was a moment when a woman's soul is more incarnate than at any other time; when the most spiritual beauty bespeaks itself flesh; and sex takes the outside place in the presentation.

Then those eyes flashed brightly through their filmy heaviness before the remainder of her face was well awake. With an oddly compounded look of gladness, shyness, and surprise, she exclaimed –

'O Mr. Clare! How you frightened me – I –'

There had not at first been time for her to think of the changed relations which his declaration had introduced; but the full sense of the matter rose up in her face when she encountered Clare's tender look as he stepped forward to the bottom stair.

'Dear, darling Tessy!' he whispered, putting his arm round her, and his face to her flushed cheek. 'Don't, for Heaven's sake, Mister me any more. I have hastened back so soon because of you!'

Tess's excitable heart beat against his by way of reply; and there they stood upon the red-brick floor of the entry, the sun slanting in by the window upon his back, as he held her tightly to his breast; upon her inclining face, upon the blue veins of her temple, upon her naked arm, and her neck, and into the depths of her hair. Having been lying down in her clothes she was warm as a sunned cat. At first she would not look straight up at him, but her eyes soon lifted, and his plumbed the deepness of the ever-varying pupils, with their radiating fibrils of blue, and black, and gray, and violet, while she regarded him as Eve at her second waking might have regarded Adam.

'I've got to go a-skimming,' she pleaded, 'and I have on'y old Deb to help me to-day. Mrs. Crick is gone to market with Mr. Crick, and Retty is not well, and the others are gone out somewhere, and won't be home till milking.'

As they retreated to the milk-house Deborah Fyander appeared on the stairs.

'I have come back, Deborah,' said Mr. Clare, upwards. 'So I can help Tess with the skimming; and, as you are very tired, I am sure, you needn't come down till milking-time.'

Possibly the Talbothays milk was not very thoroughly skimmed that afternoon. Tess was in a dream wherein familiar objects appeared as having light and shade and position, but no particular outline. Every time she held the skimmer under the pump to cool it for the work her hand trembled, the ardour of his affection being so palpable that she seemed to flinch under it like a plant in too burning a sun.

Then he pressed her again to his side, and when she had done running her forefinger round the leads to cut off the cream-edge, he cleaned it in nature's way; for the unconstrained manner of Talbothays dairy came convenient now.

'I may as well say it now as later, dearest,' he resumed gently. 'I wish to ask you something of a very practical nature, which I have been thinking of ever since that day last week in the meads. I shall soon want to marry, and, being a farmer, you see I shall require for my wife a woman who knows all about the management of farms. Will you be that woman, Tessy?'

He put it in that way that she might not think he had yielded to an impulse of which his head would disapprove.

She turned quite careworn. She had bowed to the inevitable result of proximity, the necessity of loving him; but she had not calculated upon this sudden corollary, which, indeed, Clare had put before her without quite meaning himself to do it so soon. With pain that was like the bitterness of dissolution she murmured the words of her indispensable and worn answer as an honourable woman.

'O Mr. Clare – I cannot be your wife – I cannot be!'

The sound of her own decision seemed to break Tess's very heart, and she bowed her face in her grief.

'But, Tess!' he said, amazed at her reply, and holding her still more greedily close. 'Do you say no? Surely you love me?'

'O yes, yes! And I would rather be yours than anybody's in the world,' returned the sweet and honest voice of the distressed girl. 'But I *cannot* marry you!'

'Tess,' he said, holding her at arm's length, 'you are engaged to marry some one else!'

'No, no!'

'Then why do you refuse me?'

'I don't want to marry! I have not thought of doing it. I cannot! I only want to love you.'

'But why?'

Driven to subterfuge, she stammered –

'Your father is a parson, and your mother wouldn' like you to marry such as me. She will want you to marry a lady.'

'Nonsense – I have spoken to them both. That was partly why I went home.'

'I feel I cannot – never, never!' she echoed.

'Is it too sudden to be asked thus, my Pretty?'

'Yes – I did not expect it.'

'If you will let it pass, please, Tessy, I will give you time,' he said. 'It was very abrupt to come home and speak to you all at once. I'll not allude to it again for a while.'

She again took up the shining skimmer, held it beneath the pump, and began anew. But she could not, as at other times, hit the exact under-surface of the cream with the delicate dexterity required, try as she might: sometimes she was cutting down into the milk, sometimes in the air. She could hardly see, her eyes having filled with two blurring tears drawn forth by a grief which, to this her best friend and dear advocate, she could never explain.

**COMMENTARY**

**1** Notice the negative formulation of the opening sentence, 'Not a human being . . .' which focuses attention on the natural world. The 'denizens' (people who live and work there) are symbolised by their pails hanging out to dry. A note of humour is introduced by juxtaposing the 'sustained snores' of the sleeping humans with the 'grunt and squeal of sweltering pigs'. A fanciful note is also introduced by the transference of the verb 'slept' to the rhubarb and the cabbages. All this conjures up a bucolic atmosphere (sights and sounds of contented rural life).

The third paragraph also creates vivid impressions. The theme of sleepiness continues but there are sharp observations to match the pails, the pigs and the vegetable patch in paragraph one. Notice: 'the red interior of her mouth'; 'her coiled-up cable of hair'; 'stretched one arm'; 'face . . . flushed . . . eyelids heavy'. But these observations are being made in Hardy's imagination, and subsequently in every reader's imagination. As a consequence the factual details are transformed by metaphors that also lie in the imagination. Tess's arm isn't really 'satin', nor is she really a 'brim-full' cup or bowl with fumes of 'nature' breathing from her. Yet the reader responds to all this because language works so effectively in mixtures of the literal and the metaphorical. The sentence that concludes this paragraph is rhapsodic in the way that it sums up the moment. It is full of abstractions: 'a woman's soul'; 'spiritual beauty'; and the final statement, sounding slightly odd to a modern reader, 'sex takes the outside place in the presentation'. Note too the use of words such as 'incarnate' and 'bespeaks itself flesh' with which Hardy refers explicitly to the idea of giving body to abstract or 'spiritual' concepts.

**2** Throughout the excerpt there are references to physical aspects of humans and their behaviour. Here are some examples:
*snoring; the touch of a descending foot; her mouth; stretched . . . arm; cable of hair; satin delicacy above the sunburn; face . . . flushed; eyelids hung heavy; eyes flashed; her face was well awake; putting his arm round her; flushed cheek; excitable heart beat; the blue veins of her temple; naked arm; neck; warm as a sunned cat; ever-varying pupils, with their radiating fibrils of blue, and black, and gray, and violet; her hand trembled, the ardour of his affection being so palpable; he pressed her again to his side and when she had done running her forefinger round the leads to cut off the cream-edge, he cleaned it in nature's way;* and so on.

**3** Given the sensuous, physicality of much of the preceding description, Angel Clare's proposal seems oddly businesslike. A little earlier, Hardy writes, almost anticipating the soft-focus camera technique of the ITV production:

'Tess was in a dream wherein familiar objects appeared as having light and shade and position, but no particular outline.'

Clare's proposal shatters this romantic dreamworld for Tess. Her sense of shame (the convention of the day) means that she must reject a proposal which could have united romance and practicality in a new, happy life. Note how Hardy describes this realisation as 'pain that was like the bitterness of dissolution'. The effects created by the lexis of the preceding, continuous description does in fact dissolve into the lexis of distressed conversation:

questions; exclamations; denials; negatives; stammering; apology.

4 As stated above, the artistic effect of the conversation after the proposal is to dispel a dreamworld and plunge the reader into the interactions of an ill-fated relationship. Hardy employs a number of features of real-life conversations in order to make it believable. Note the following:

- 'O Mr Clare . . .' (exclamation followed by uncompleted/interrupted sentence)
- 'Dear, darling Tessy . . . Don't . . . Mister me any more' (endearments and diminutive form of address, rejecting formality)
- 'a-skimming' (dialect expression)
- 'on'y old Deb' (phonetic representation plus another diminutive term of reference)
- 'I may as well say it now as later . . .' (common opening strategy for something difficult to say)
- 'I cannot be' (repetition – note use of italics for this word later to give further emphasis)
- 'O Mr Clare – I cannot be your wife – I cannot be' (dashes are used to indicate discontinuity in speech)
- 'Will you be that woman, Tessy?' (this is the first of seven questions asked by Angel Clare (one is implied, 'you are engaged . . .')
- 'I cannot . . .' (the first of twelve denials or negatives uttered by Tess)
- 'I will not allude to it again for a while' (to all intents and purposes the conversation is at an end, rounded off by its initiator, Angel Clare).

Phonological, grammatical and pragmatic features of conversation are all exemplified here. The pragmatic feature that has tragic consequences for the novel is that Tess is unable to speak about the implication behind: 'I would rather be yours than anybody's in the world'. Angel is left disappointed and uncomprehending despite the fact that they have 'communicated'.

One of the distinctive features of prose fiction is the way in which language can be used imaginatively to give unspoken meanings (thought) equal prominence with spoken meanings. Perceiving contradictory or contrasting meanings accounts for that sense of tragic irony or bizarre comedy that readers enjoy in classic tales. It is also a notable feature of TV productions in which camera close-ups contrast with the words spoken.

# Poems on the Underground

One rough and ready, but useful, way of sorting out the written language in our lives, is to classify it into texts that you go looking for because you need them (dictionaries, maps, telephone directories, reference books) or want them (newspapers, magazines, 'light reading'), and texts that come looking for you (bills, income tax returns, letters, junk mail). You could say that there are also texts that lie in wait for you in waiting rooms, on display stands or on public hoardings.

There is also the Internet which you can choose to surf without necessarily having a purpose. A term sometimes used to refer to this kind of chance discovery or unexpected encounter is serendipity.

Poetry is sometimes discovered by serendipity, though it can also be encountered in a 'set book'. It is a minority of readers who regularly seek out poetry, especially new poetry, for the curiosity and the pleasure of reading it. True, there are special occasions – a wedding, a celebration, or writing a love letter – when people try to find or even write 'a bit of poetry' to suit the occasion. The appearance of a poem in the Aldwych Underground station in London, on Wednesday 29 January, 1986, marked a new venture in bringing poetry texts to the public. Nothing was being advertised, the whole enterprise was a gift; surprises were in store.

With financial assistance from the Arts Council and two publishers, the Compton Poetry Fund presented one hundred poems to an unsuspecting public, displaying them on London Underground trains. Here are some things the organisers had to say in the anthology that was eventually published:

> Anyone who suffers from an addiction to reading cereal box tops or bus tickets will understand the special appeal of *Poems on the Underground* . . . how pleasant it would be, we thought, to read a few lines by one's favourite poet on the Tube, instead of advertisements for mints and temps.
>
> When we began to scatter poems about in public, we had no idea how people would respond . . . The truth, as we soon discovered, is that England is a nation of poetry-lovers. Hundreds of people wrote in . . . many letters just said, in effect, 'Thank you, whoever you are, for the poems'.

You now have an opportunity to look at three of the poems displayed on Underground trains. The first poem is *Ozymandias* by Percy Bysshe Shelley, the second, *Composed Upon Westminster Bridge, September 3, 1802*, by William Wordsworth, the third, *Holy Sonnet*, by John Donne.

## ACTIVITY 6

Read *Ozymandias*, giving consideration to the following questions:

1. How many people are there in the poem, and who is addressing whom?
2. How many sentences are there, and what do you notice about their construction? Look, for example, at the length.
3. Do you notice any patterning of words and ideas?
4. Do you notice any semantic field(s) formed by words in the poem?
5. What do you notice about the sounds and rhythm of the poem? Ensure that you actually listen to the poem read aloud by you or somebody else.

## *Ozymandias by Percy Bysshe Shelley (1792–1822)*

I met a traveller from an antique land
Who said: Two vast and trunkless legs of stone
Stand in the desert. Near them, on the sand,
Half sunk, a shattered visage lies, whose frown,
And wrinkled lip, and sneer of cold command,
Tell that its sculptor well those passions read
Which yet survive, stamped on these lifeless things,
The hand that mocked them and the heart that fed;
And on the pedestal these words appear:
"My name is Ozymandias, king of kings:
Look on my works, ye Mighty, and despair!"
Nothing beside remains. Round the decay
Of that colossal wreck, boundless and bare
The lone and level sands stretch far away.

**COMMENTARY**

1 The poem begins in exactly the same way that many casual conversations might begin: 'I met this bloke, and he said . . .' or 'I met a woman from somewhere or other, and she said to me . . .'. The poem is in no way lessened by observing this commonplace occurrence. It is a strategy that establishes a storyteller, the 'I' of the poem, and an implied listener, 'you'. The 'I' need not be Shelley, it can be a role adopted by the writer, just as the 'you' need not necessarily be you personally. Thus, between you the reader and Shelley the poet, there is a little group of people being constructed: the traveller and the person being spoken to, a sculptor and Ozymandias himself, either as a historical person or as a broken statue. The obviously direct speech in the poem consists of Ozymandias' words, ironically in the form of an inscription carved by the sculptor. The form of the speech is a statement followed by a command (or imperative) that echoes the 'sneer of cold command' in line five. Ozymandias' words are embedded in the direct speech of the traveller – speech within a speech. Ironically, Ozymandias' words have survived partly through the traveller's tale, but mainly through the enduring writing in stone of an anonymous sculptor who was not even one of the 'mighty' addressed by Ozymandias.

2 The sentence structure is worth noting as evidence of how poetry, in its original meaning, is a matter of making or crafting something in words. The first sentence ends in the middle of the third line, the last begins in the middle of the third line from the end. Coincidence? Both sentences contain exactly twenty four syllables if you pronounce 'traveller' as 'trav'ler' as most people do. Another coincidence? The second sentence is a long one with a spoken sentence embedded within it. Notice the eight commas, the semi-colon and the two colons. That much punctuation is asking to be read aloud. Shelley was as aware as Dickens of the dramatic effect of a very short sentence following a very long one. There are only three words in the third sentence, which, when spoken aloud at a steady pace, has an extremely resonant effect. Part of the resonance is created by the combination of particular vowels and

nasal sounds: 'Nothing' and 'remains'. Nasal sounds can of course sound whining, but not here because of the effect of gravitas created by three two-syllable words forming a sentence that sounds epigrammatic, the last word, a judgement on Ozymandias' own words.

**3** Close inspection reveals a number of patternings that provide evidence of the disciplined concern for form that characterises verse. Here are some examples:

- notice the bound, final morpheme occurring three times (trunkless, lifeless, boundless)
- notice the contrast of 'Near them, on the sand' at the beginning and 'sands stretch far away' at the end. Coincidence? Intended? Or the subconscious instinct of a fine poet?
- notice the nice balance of 'The hand that mocked them and the heart that fed'.

**4** The most obvious semantic field is one of destruction: trunkless; shattered; nothing ... remains; decay; wreck; bare. There is also a semantic field of body references, appropriate to a poem about a sculpture: trunkless legs; visage; lip; hand; heart; pedestal (support for feet and thus for whole of the statue). At the word 'pedestal' the semantic field for body ends suddenly and the remaining lines tell of a vain inscription and the vast, empty desert.

You can also discern a theme of negativity or loss: trunkless; half sunk; lifeless things; despair; Nothing; boundless and bare; lone.

Reference has already been made to the gravitas (weight and seriousness) achieved by the rhythm. The lines are all evenly decasyllabic which makes them approximate to a familiar speech rhythm (You boil the kettle, I'll lay the table) – the iambic pentameter. The sheer regularity of this rhythm, and the presence of rhymes and assonance (repeated or very similar vowel sounds) are hallmarks of poetic crafting that one would not normally expect in speech or written prose. The regularity does not lead to monotony because of the variations in rhyme and assonance. There is some alliteration (stone/stand; sand/sunk; cold/command; boundless/bare; lone/level). Alliteration is not difficult to discover (initial consonant rhyming). Used subtly, it can create a pleasing effect but do not forget that in a language that uses half a million or so words and has only 28 spoken consonants (21 written ones) much alliteration is accidental rather than intentional. Nevertheless, readers would probably agree that there is a musicality in the poem's arrangement of sounds which makes it memorable.

## *Composed Upon Westminster Bridge, September 3, 1802 by William Wordsworth (1770–1850)*

**ACTIVITY 7**

Now look at the poem below. Read it a few times (aloud as well as silently) and consider the following:

1. How many people are there in the poem? Compare this with *Ozymandias*. Who is being addressed?
2. How many sentences does it consist of, and how are they structured? Note the punctuation.
3. What rhythm and sounds do you detect in the poem?
4. What is the poem about? How is it different in subject from *Ozymandias*?

## Composed upon Westminster Bridge, September 3, 1802

Earth has not anything to show more fair:
Dull would he be of soul who could pass by
A sight so touching in its majesty:
This City now doth like a garment wear
The beauty of the morning; silent, bare,
Ships, towers, domes, theatres, and temples lie
Open unto the fields, and to the sky;
All bright and glittering in the smokeless air.
Never did sun more beautifully steep
In his first splendour valley, rock, or hill;
Ne'er saw I, never felt, a calm so deep!
The river glideth at his own sweet will:
Dear God! the very houses seem asleep;
And all that mighty heart is lying still!

**COMMENTARY**

1. The poem moves in a series of third person statements until it reaches the 'I' in line 11. In line 13, the 'I' addresses God, 'Dear God!'. There is as much stage setting in the details of the language here as there is in *Ozymandias* (line six, for example, is a list of details), but it is much more a single person poem, musing on the beauty of a scene. It sounds like an outburst of song, and it ends with an exclamation mark, as do Ozymandias' words. The meaning of the term 'lyric poetry' is ideally illustrated here: a song-poem directed at nobody in particular, for anyone to hear who wishes to do so.
2. There are three sentences, the first more than half the poem in length (eight lines). The punctuation keeps the sense tidy but enables the outpouring to run free. In the last six lines there is a rising cry of exclamation expressed in the accumulating 'never', 'Ne'er,' 'never' and reinforced by three exclamation marks.
3. Again, the metre favoured is the decasyllabic line. Alliteration is not a feature of the poem but assonance, a much more subtle business, is very effective. Say to yourself the last three words of each line, one line after the other and you will hear the music in the words.

The two poems contrast very strongly in their language functions.

Wordsworth's poem celebrates a breathtaking moment of revelation. The semantic field is one of optimism and joy:

fair; touching; majesty; beauty; bright and glimmering; beautifully; splendour; calm; sweet; mighty heart.

Contrast this with Ozymandias, a poem about vanity:

shattered visage; frown; wrinkled; lifeless; mocked; despair; Nothing ... remains decay; bare; lone.

Note too that whereas Ozymandias has an unspecified timelessness, Wordsworth's poem is quite precisely dated. Even the time of day is quite clear.

## *The difference two syllables can make*

Side by side are an excerpt from Wordsworth's *Resolution and Independence* and a satire on the Wordsworth poem by Lewis Carroll, *Upon The Lonely Moor*. Carroll deliberately takes (for his day) a modern, jocular tone to poke fun at the solemn diction used by Wordsworth, but notice especially what a difference the loss of two syllables makes. Carroll's octosyllabic line is quite jaunty compared with the decasyllables of *Ozymandias* and the lines of *Westminster Bridge*.

### RESOLUTION AND INDEPENDENCE

A gentle answer did the old Man make,
In courteous speech which forth he slowly drew:
And him with further words I thus bespake,
'What occupation do you there pursue?
This is a lonesome place for one like you.'
Ere he replied, a flash of mild surprise
Broke from the sable orbs of his yet-vivid eyes.

His words came feebly, from a feeble chest,
But each in solemn order followed each,
With something of a lofty utterance drest –
Choice word and measured phrase, above the reach
Of ordinary men; a stately speech;
Such as grave Livers do in Scotland use,
Religious men, who give to God and man their dues.

*William Wordsworth*

### UPON THE LONELY MOOR

I met an aged, aged man
Upon the lonely moor:
I knew I was a gentleman,
And he was but a boor.
So I stopped and roughly questioned him,
"Come, tell me how you live!"
But his words impressed my ear no more
Than if it were a sieve.

He said, "I look for soap-bubbles,
That lie among the wheat,
And bake them into mutton-pies,
And sell them in the street.
I sell them unto men", he said,
"Who sail on stormy seas;
And that's the way I get my bread –
A trifle, if you please."

*Lewis Carroll*

## *Holy Sonnet by John Donne (1572–1631)*

**ACTIVITY 8**

Look now at one of John Donne's *Holy Sonnets*. Read it, listen to it, and consider the following:

1 Who is addressing whom in this poem?
2 How many sentences are there and what do you notice about their function and structure?
3 What indications are there that the language here is older than Shelley's or Wordsworth's? Do you find it slightly more difficult to follow the syntax?

### Holy Sonnet

Death be not proud, though some have called thee
Mighty and dreadful, for thou art not so;
For those whom you think'st thou dost overthrow
Die not, poor death, nor yet canst thou kill me.
From rest and sleep, which but thy pictures be,
Much pleasure, then from thee much more must flow;
And soonest our best men with thee do go,
Rest of their bones, and souls' delivery.
Thou art slave to Fate, chance, kings, and desperate men.
And dost with poison, war, and sickness dwell,
And poppy or charms can make us sleep as well,
And better than thy stroke; why swell'st thou then?
One short sleep past, we wake eternally,
And death shall be no more, Death thou shalt die.

**COMMENTARY**

1 The poem addresses 'Death' using a linguistic strategy known as personification (making an abstraction seem like a person). The address is second person using the now archaic 'thee', 'thou' and 'thy'. The addresser, after an initial 'me', uses the first person plural throughout: 'our', 'us', 'we'. If the lines on *Westminster Bridge* are a personal song, Donne's poem is a voice of protest and denial on behalf, it seems, of humankind.

2 The poem is written in three four line sentences and a final two line sentence. The first sentence is a command or imperative sentence followed by a series of statements addressed to death and culminating in a rhetorical question: 'why swell'st thou then?' The last four words have an exclamatory force that echo the opening imperative: 'Death be not proud . . .'. Notice that the negative of 'be not' has been converted to positive assurance at the end, 'thou shalt'. There is considerable energy, aggression even, in the voice of this poem. This is created by the denials: 'thou art not so' and 'nor yet canst thou kill me' and the tough, insistent argumentative tone: 'poor death'; 'Thou art slave'; 'death shall be no more'. To speak to an adversary as a third person, as in 'death shall be no more' effectively robs the adversary of identity. It is not unlike the experience of being talked about as though you were not present.

3 Historical information such as the date of a text is always useful to a linguistic investigation. If nothing else it helps to confirm impressions a reader will gain from the text itself. *Westminster Bridge* and *Ozymandias* were written within 15 years of each other: 1802 and 1817, respectively. Wordsworth's poem was not published until 1807. The date for Donne's *Holy Sonnet* however is about 1610, nearly two centuries earlier. Between Donne's time and our own lie nearly four centuries of language change. The lexis of the poem contains nothing that is not common today though one or two words might be thought more likely to turn up in poetry, for example: dwell, soul, charms, eternally. Two grammatical features are very obviously not common today, the pronouns 'thee' and 'thou' and some verb forms, 'art', 'dost', 'canst', 'swell'st', 'shalt', 'thinkst'.

Unusual word order is partly accounted for by conventions in the language of Donne's own day and partly by the highly compressed nature of Donne's way of thinking and expressing himself. Try to explain the less familiar meaning of the word 'but' in the quote below.

From rest and sleep, which but thy pictures be,
Much pleasure, then from thee much more must flow;

There is a Shakespearean ring to these words. They are dramatically expressed and ask to be read aloud. A modern paraphrase might express the meaning in more familiar prose syntax, but look at what is lost in terms of verbal energy and voice:

If resting and sleeping, that resemble death, are very
enjoyable, then much more pleasure will come after death itself.

# All the world's a stage

So far in this chapter you have looked at examples of the language of prose fiction and the language of poetry. The final pair of activities are concerned with two of the best known set books in English schools, Shakespeare's *Romeo and Juliet* and Oscar Wilde's, *The Importance of Being Earnest.* Both were written for the stage and both have been translated to modern film and TV media.

## *Romeo and Juliet by William Shakespeare*

For Romeo and Juliet: One hundred free minutes of evening local calls. (Cable & Wireless advert, 1998)

### ACTIVITY 9

Read the following excerpt from *Romeo and Juliet* which depicts the first meeting of the two lovers. Ideally, you should read the excerpt aloud with a partner. Give some consideration to the following:

1 Make a flow chart of the interactions between the two speakers. You could note such things as when speech is an aside? Who asks a question? When? Find a word or two that will summarise the purpose of each speech.
2 Trace through the text references to speaking and swearing a vow. What seems to be at issue?
3 What significance is given to names?
4 The mixture of love and poetry generates a remarkable range of fanciful ideas and extravagent expression. Note some of these. Look for similes and metaphors.
5 Examine the linguistic evidence that an argument is in fact taking place as well as declarations of love.

ROMEO [*coming forward*]
*[Enter Juliet above at a window.]*
But soft! What light through yonder window breaks?
It is the East, and Juliet is the sun!
Arise, fair sun, and kill the envious moon,
Who is already sick and pale with grief
That thou her maid art far more fair than she.
Be not her maid, since she is envious.
Her vestal livery is but sick and green,
And none but fools do wear it. Cast it off.

It is my lady; O, it is my love!
O that she knew she were!
She speaks, yet she says nothing. What of that?
Her eye discourses; I will answer it.
I am too bold; 'tis not to me she speaks.
Two of the fairest stars in all the heaven,
Having some business, do entreat her eyes
To twinkle in their spheres till they return.
What if her eyes were there, they in her head?
The brightness of her cheek would shame those stars
As daylight doth a lamp; her eyes in heaven
Would through the airy region stream so bright
That birds would sing and think it were not night.
See how she leans her cheek upon her hand!
O that I were a glove upon that hand,
That I might touch that cheek!

JULIET
Ay me!

ROMEO
She speaks.
O, speak again, bright angel! for thou art
As glorious to this night, being o'er my head,
As is a wingèd messenger of heaven
Unto the white-upturnèd wond'ring eyes
Of mortals that fall back to gaze on him
When he bestrides the lazy-pacing clouds
And sails upon the bosom of the air.

JULIET
O Romeo, Romeo! wherefore art thou Romeo?
Deny thy father and refuse thy name;
Or, if thou wilt not, be but sworn my love,
And I'll no longer be a Capulet.

ROMEO *[aside]*
Shall I hear more, or shall I speak at this?

JULIET
'Tis but thy name that is my enemy.
Thou art thyself, though not a Montague.
What's Montague? It is nor hand, nor foot,
Nor arm, nor face, nor any other part
Belonging to a man. O, be some other name!
What's in a name? That which we call a rose
By any other name would smell as sweet.
So Romeo would, were he not Romeo called,
Retain that dear perfection which he owes
Without that title. Romeo, doff thy name;
And for thy name, which is no part of thee,
Take all myself.

ROMEO
I take thee at thy word.
Call me but love, and I'll be new baptized;
Henceforth I never will be Romeo

JULIET
What man art thou that, thus bescreened in night,
So stumblest on my counsel?

ROMEO
By a name
I know not how to tell thee who I am.
My name, dear saint, is hateful to myself,
Because it is an enemy to thee.
Had I it written, I would tear the word.

JULIET
My ears have yet not drunk a hundred words
Of thy tongue's uttering, yet I know the sound.
Art thou not Romeo, and a Montague?

ROMEO
Neither, fair maid, if either thee dislike.

JULIET
How camest thou hither, tell me, and wherefore?
The orchard walls are high and hard to climb,
And the place death, considering who thou art,
If any of my kinsmen find thee here.

ROMEO
With love's light wings did I o'erperch these walls;
For stony limits cannot hold love out,
And what love can do, that dares love attempt.
Therefore thy kinsmen are no stop to me.

JULIET
If they do see thee, they will murder thee.

ROMEO
Alack, there likes more peril in thine eye
Than twenty of their swords! Look thou but sweet,
And I am proof against their enmity.

JULIET
I would not for the world they saw thee here.

ROMEO
I have night's cloak to hide me from their eyes;
And but thou love me, let them find me here.
My life were better ended by their hate
Than death proroguèd, wanting of thy love.

JULIET
By whose direction found'st thou out this place?

ROMEO
By love, that first did prompt me to inquire.
He lent me counsel, and I lent him eyes.
I am no pilot; yet, wert thou as far
As that vast shore washed with the farthest sea,
I should adventure for such merchandise.

JULIET
Thou knowest the mask of night is on my face;
Else would a maiden blush bepaint my cheek
For that which thou hast heard me speak to-night.
Fain would I dwell on form – fain, fain deny
What I have spoke; but farewell compliment!
Dost thou love me? I know thou wilt say 'Ay';
And I will take thy word. Yet, if thou swear'st,
Thou mayst prove false. At lovers' perjuries,
They say Jove laughs. O gentle Romeo,
If thou dost love, pronounce it faithfully.
Or if thou thinkest I am too quickly won,
I'll frown, and be perverse, and say thee nay,
So thou wilt woo; but else, not for the world.
In truth, fair Montague, I am too fond,
And therefore thou mayst think my havior light;
But trust me, gentleman, I'll prove more true
Than those that have more cunning to be strange.
I should have been more strange, I must confess,
But that thou overheard'st, ere I was ware,
My true-love passion. Therefore pardon me,
And not impute this yielding to light love,
Which the dark night hath so discoverèd.

ROMEO
Lady, by yonder blessèd moon I vow,
That tips with silver all these fruit-tree tops –
JULIET
O, swear not by the moon, th' inconstant moon,
That monthly changes in her circled orb,
Lest that thy love prove likewise variable.
ROMEO
What shall I swear by?
JULIET Do not swear at all;
Or if thou wilt, swear by thy gracious self,
Which is the god of my idolatry,
And I'll believe thee.
ROMEO If my heart's dear love –
JULIET
Well, do not swear. Although I joy in thee,
I have no joy of this contract to-night.
It is too rash, too unadvised, too sudden;
Too like the lightning, which doth cease to be
Ere one can say 'It lightens.' Sweet, good night!
This bud of love, by summer's ripening breath,
May prove a beauteous flow'r when next we meet.
Good night, good night! As sweet repose and rest
Come to thy heart as that within my breast!
ROMEO
O, wilt thou leave me so unsatisified?
JULIET
What satisfaction canst thou have to-night?
ROMEO
Th' exchange of thy love's faithful vow for mine.
JULIET
I gave thee mine before thou didst request it;
And yet I would it were to give again.
ROMEO
Wouldst thou withdraw it? For what purpose, love?
JULIET
But to be frank and give it thee again.
And yet I wish but for the thing I have.
My bounty is as boundless as the sea,
My love as deep; the more I give to thee,
The more I have, for both are infinite.
I hear some noise within. Dear love, adieu!
*[Nurse calls within.]*
Anon, good nurse! Sweet Montague, be true.
Stay but a little, I will come again. *[Exit.]*
ROMEO
O blessèd, blessèd night! I am afeard,
Being in night, all this is but a dream,
Too flattering-sweet to be substantial.
*[Enter Juliet above.]*
JULIET
Three words, dear Romeo, and good night indeed.
If that thy bent of love be honorable,
Thy purpose marriage, send me word to-morrow,
By one that I'll procure to come to thee,
Where and what time thou wilt perform the rite;
And all my fortunes at thy foot I'll lay
And follow thee my lord throughout the world.
NURSE *[within]* Madam!
JULIET
I come, anon. – But if thou meanest not well,
I do beseech thee –
NURSE *[within]*
Madam!
JULIET By and by I come. –
To cease thy suit and leave me to my grief.
To-morrow will I send.
ROMEO So thrive my soul –
JULIET
A thousand times good night! *[Exit.]*
ROMEO
A thousand times the worse, to want thy light!
Love goes toward love as schoolboys from their books;
But love from love, toward school with heavy looks.
*Enter Juliet [above] again.*
JULIET
Hist! Romeo, hist! O for a falc'ner's voice
To lure this tassel-gentle back again!
Bondage is hoarse and may not speak aloud,
Else would I tear the cave where Echo lies
And make her airy tongue more hoarse than mine
With repetition of 'My Romeo!'
ROMEO
It is my soul that calls upon my name.
How silver-sweet sound lovers' tongues by night,
Like softest music to attending ears!
JULIET
Romeo!
ROMEO My sweet?
JULIET At what o'clock to-morrow
Shall I send to thee?
ROMEO By the hour of nine.
JULIET
I will not fail. 'Tis twenty years till then.
I have forgot why I did call thee back.
ROMEO
Let me stand here till thou remember it.
JULIET
I shall forget, to have thee still stand there,
Rememb'ring how I love thy company.
ROMEO
And I'll still stay, to have thee still forget,
Forgetting any other home but this.
JULIET
'Tis almost morning. I would have thee gone –
And yet no farther than a wanton's bird,
That lets it hop a little from her hand,
Like a poor prisoner in his twisted gyves,
And with a silken thread plucks it back again,
So loving-jealous of his liberty.
ROMEO
I would I were thy bird.

JULIET Sweet, so would I.
Yet I should kill thee with much cherishing.
Good night, good night! Parting is such sweet sorrow
That I shall say good night till it be morrow. [Exit.]

ROMEO
Sleep dwell upon thine eyes, peace in thy breast!
Would I were sleep and peace, so sweet to rest!
Hence will I to my ghostly father's cell,
His help to crave and my dear hap to tell. *Exit.*

**1** Romeo is alone, talking to himself, or, more accurately, thinking aloud for the benefit of an audience. The convention whereby actors address two audiences (one on the stage, the other in the auditorium) will be discussed later. Juliet, also alone and standing at her window, is also deep in private thoughts. Her exclamation seems like a sigh.

Romeo urges her to speak though there is no acknowledgement of each other's presence. Juliet, still thinking aloud, expresses regret that their very names should get in the way of their love.

Romeo speaks an aside which tells the 'other audience' what he is thinking. Juliet asks, 'What's in a name? and declares her love. This is a cue for Romeo to reveal himself and declare his love. There follows a series of exchanges in which Juliet asks four questions and also expresses anxiety about being discovered. The characters are now addressing each other directly, albeit at a distance and in the dark.

Juliet then speaks at length. She realises that her heartfelt declaration has been overheard and might be misunderstood as only 'light love'.

Romeo's vow (presumably of true love in return) is immediately interrupted by Juliet. Romeo then asks by what he may swear his love and Juliet tells him not to swear a vow at all. As Romeo is about to reply, Juliet interrupts him again. Her anxiety about the suddenness of their love prompts her to bid him a fond good night.

Romeo protests with a question to which Juliet replies with a question. The play on the word 'satisfaction' is a light joke that a late twentieth century reader can still share with a late 16th century audience.

Romeo then asks two more questions and Juliet replies, reassuringly in one sense, but playfully in another. Notice the need to round off a conversation one way or another. Juliet does it with the Elizabethan equivalent of, 'I think there's somebody coming'.

**2** Reflections on the nature of language and the pragmatics of its spoken forms are never very far away from Shakespeare's mind. He was an instinctive linguistic observer. The note is first struck by Romeo's words:

She speaks, yet says nothing; what of that?
Her eye discourses, I will answer it.

Her words don't say what he would like to hear, but her eyes do. Everybody knows what that means, innocently or knowingly. A strong semantic field in his opening speech, however, is noticeable: eyes, head, cheek (three times), hand. 'O that I were a glove upon that hand'. There is physical passion as well as poetic imagery in the language of that first speech. A little later, speaking is referred to twice more, and hearing once.

Juliet's question, 'What's in a name?' and her own answer, 'That which we call a rose / By any other word would smell as sweet' have echoed through the centuries. The tragic answer is that names will bring about Romeo and Juliet's deaths. For it is the total unacceptability of Juliet ever becoming Mrs Montague that dooms their love: ' 'Tis but thy name that is my enemy'.

With this sort of instinctive understanding it is not surprising that Juliet advises caution with a hint of scepticism when it comes to another fact of language – that vows are only words, and nothing like as binding or inescapable as names. Vowing and naming are both speech acts with significant consequences. With naming, the recipient can do little about it; vows on the other hand are action in the form of intention. Romeo is all for swearing an eternal vow while Juliet is sure of her love but less sure about vows. Notice that in her longest speech she expresses considerable doubt about the very words of love, let alone *vows* of love:

Dost thou love me? I know thou wilt say, 'Ay',
And I will take thy word; yet if thou swear'st,
Thou may'st prove false . . .
If thou dost love, pronounce it faithfully.

Only names seem to be permanent and reliable, however 'star crossed'; vows are too finite for a love which is 'infinite'.

**3** The significance of names has already been discussed because it is a topic interwoven with vows and the way in which language both constrains us (by our names, for example) and sets us free to declare love and make vows.

It is interesting to note that names play a significant part in all the texts you have looked at so far. The graveyard surname Dickens gives to the schoolmaster, Headstone, for example, is not accidental. If you choose to read *Our Mutual Friend*, or saw the TV version, you will also know that one character conceals his true name and identity until he knows that he is truly loved for himself.

*Tess of the D'Urbervilles* is entitled with the very surname that precipitates Tess' tragic life, since she is encouraged by her impoverished family to claim kinship with a wealthier branch of the family. Ironically, it turns out that Alec D'Urberville had merely adopted the name and is not of noble descent after all.

*Ozymandias* is another name to be reckoned with. It is the Greek form for the Ancient Egyptian name, Rameses.

After you have finished this activity you will be looking at a play by Oscar Wilde which contains a character masquerading under the name of Ernest, rather than his true name, Jack.

**4** One way of thinking about the rich poetic texture of this scene is to visualise a picture that contains not only the characters and the setting of the scene (window, garden, moonlight), but also the symbols and images in the language: sun, stars, winged messenger of heaven, greenness, a lamp, birds, bosom of the air, upturned eyes, puffing clouds, a rose, orchard walls, wings, swords, the sea and its shore, maiden blush, silver, fruit trees, breast. All this makes pretty good, traditional Valentine card material. There is also language that does its best to say what seems impossible:

My bounty is as boundless as the sea,
My love is deep; the more I give to thee,
The more I have, for both are infinite.

Self-contradictory statements of this kind are known as paradoxes. You may have noticed a paradox earlier, in Donne's poem, *Death Be Not Proud*, in which the poet says that those who die, do not in fact die but that death itself will die.

A semantic field you may have detected in the Shakespeare text seems to run counter to the yearnings and protestations of romantic love. Words such as: 'merchandise', 'contract', 'exchange' and 'withdraw' create a metaphor to do with trade and legality. It's a thin thread of metaphor but it is there nevertheless, and links the hard reality of names to the more uncertain reality of vows.

**5** Whilst this excerpt is universally regarded as a classic scene of romantic love, the language isn't just concerned with hearts and flowers. It has the same tenacious, argumentative quality of the Donne poem, written 15 or so years later.

The opening speech begins with a 'But ...' expressing caution though, essentially, the speech is one long exclamation: 'O, it is my love ... O that she knew she were ... O that I were a glove'.

The argument may be said to begin with Juliet's self-questioning 'wherefore art thou Romeo?' and 'What's in a name?' Running with this is a preoccupation with the power of some words, and the possible fragility of vows. Romeo says of his name, 'Had I it written, I would tear the word' and Juliet follows this immediately with, 'My ears have not yet drunk a hundred words / Of thy tongue's uttering...'. Romeo is intensely concerned to find words to vow his love; Juliet, equally in love, accepts that true love is unspeakable but no less true.

When you have completed this activity, look again at the line: 'Her eye discourses.' Investigate the word 'discourses' as used here and compare it with the use of the word in a modern A-Level syllabus.

## *The Importance of Being Earnest by Oscar Wilde*

### ACTIVITY 10

Look now at the excerpt from *The Importance of Being Earnest* written exactly 300 years after *Romeo and Juliet*. Both are love stories, one a tragedy, the other a comedy. Both excerpts are private scenes, out of earshot of adults or anyone with a say in the lovers' future happiness. Both, oddly enough, raise the question, 'What's in a name?' Jack, for complicated and comic reasons, calls himself Ernest when in town, and the woman he loves, Gwendolen, believes his name to be Ernest. Gwendolen's mother, Lady Bracknell, has gone into the music room and Jack/Ernest seizes the opportunity to propose.

Read the excerpt, at least once aloud, preferably with a partner so that you can act it out.

**Jack**. Charming day it has been, Miss Fairfax.
**Gwendolen**. Pray don't talk to me about the weather, Mr. Worthing. Whenever people talk to me about the weather, I always feel quite certain that they mean something else. And that makes me so nervous.
**Jack**. I do mean something else.
**Gwendolen**. I thought so. In fact, I am never wrong.
**Jack**. And I would like to be allowed to take advantage of Lady Bracknell's temporary absence ...
**Gwendolen**. I would certainly advise you to do so. Mama has a way of coming back suddenly into a room that I have often had to speak to her about.
**Jack**. (*nervously*). Miss Fairfax, ever since I met you I have admired you more than any girl ... I have ever met since ... I met you.
**Gwendolen**. Yes, I am quite aware of the fact. And I often wish that in public, at any rate, you had been more demonstrative. For me you have always had an irresistible fascination. Even before I met you I was far from indifferent to you. (*JACK looks at her in amazement.*) We live, as I hope you know, Mr. Worthing, in an age of ideals. The fact is constantly mentioned in the more expensive monthly magazines, and has reached the provincial pulpits, I am told; and my ideal has always been to love someone of the name of Ernest. There is something in that name that inspires absolute confidence. The moment Algernon first mentioned to me that he had a friend called Ernest, I knew I was destined to love you.
**Jack**. You really love me, Gwendolen?
**Gwendolen**. Passionately!
**Jack**. Darling! You don't know how happy you've made me.
**Gwendolen**. My own Ernest!
**Jack**. But you don't really mean to say that you couldn't love me if my name wasn't Ernest?
**Gwendolen**. But your name is Ernest.
**Jack**. Yes. I know it is. But supposing it was something else? Do you mean to say you couldn't love me then?
**Gwendolen**. (*glibly*). Ah! That is clearly a metaphysical speculation, and like most metaphysical speculations has very little reference at all to the actual facts of real life, as we know them.
**Jack**. Personally, darling, to speak quite candidly, I don't much care about the name of Ernest. ... I don't think the name suits me at all.
**Gwendolen**. It suits you perfectly. It is a divine name. It has a music of its own. It produces vibrations.
**Jack**. Well, really, Gwendolen, I must say that I think there are lots of other much nicer names. I think Jack, for instance, a charming name.
**Gwendolen**. Jack? ... No, there is very little music in the name Jack, if any at all, indeed. It does not thrill. It produces absolutely no vibrations. ... I have known several Jacks, and they all, without exception, were more than usually plain. Besides, Jack is a notorious domesticity for John! And I pity any woman who is married to a man called John. She would probably never be allowed to know the entrancing pleasure of a single moment's solitude. The only really safe name is Ernest.
**Jack**. Gwendolen, I must get christened at once – I mean we must get married at once. There is no time to be lost.
**Gwendolen**. Married, Mr. Worthing?
**Jack**. (*astounded*). Well ... surely. You know that I love you, and you led me to believe, Miss Farfax, that you were not absolutely indifferent to me.
**Gwendolen**. I adore you. But you haven't proposed to me yet. Nothing has been said at all about marriage. The subject has not even been touched on.
**Jack**. Well ... may I propose to you now?
**Gwendolen**. I think it would be an admirable opportunity. And to spare you any possible disappointment, Mr. Worthing, I think it only fair to tell you quite frankly beforehand that I am fully determined to accept you.
**Jack**. Gwendolen!
**Gwendolen**. Yes, Mr. Worthing, what have you got to say to me?
**Jack**. You know what I have got to say to you.
**Gwendolen**. Yes, but you don't say it.
**Jack.** (*goes on his knees*). Gwendolen, will you marry me?
**Gwendolen**. Of course I will, darling. How long have you been about it! I am afraid you have had very little experience in how to propose.
**Jack**. My own one, I have never loved anyone in the world but you.
**Gwendolen**. Yes, but men often propose for practice. I know my brother Gerald does. All my girlfriends tell me so. What wonderfully blue eyes you have, Ernest! They are quite, quite blue. I hope you will always look at me just like that, especially when there are other people present.
[*Enter* LADY BRACKNELL.]

Give some consideration to the following:

1 How would you describe the manner of address in this scene?
2 Bearing in mind that all the dialogue originated in the author's imagination, what is revealed of the characters of Gwendolen and Jack/Ernest by the words they have been given to speak? How far do you think the situation is as important as the characterisation?
3 Wilde does not create poetry here in the way

that Shakespeare does, but there is a relishing of the witty possibilities in the language. Identify one or two instances of wit and verbal relishing.

4 For all its farcical comedy, the excerpt is a love scene. How would you describe the differences between this scene and the one from *Romeo and Juliet?* Find words that describe the way they talk to each other and look at the sorts of words they use. Think also about pace, tone of voice, reactions to each other and social attitudes encoded in what characters say.

## COMMENTARY

**1** The conversation begins with formal terms of address: Miss Fairfax and Mr Worthing. With talk of love, first names are used, but with talk of marriage, they revert to formal address. For a while Jack uses the name Gwendolen, but she in fact remains formal until he actually makes the proposal. Then she calls him Ernest and also uses the term of endearment, 'darling' which he had used earlier.

**2** The scene is less concerned with depth of character as with social behaviour. Gwendolen actually says much more than Jack and demonstrates a much greater control over the conversation than he does. We feel that she is in charge. Her self-possession is indicated by her immediate and direct negative command, 'don't talk to me about the weather'. She further says, 'I am never wrong'.

Her longer speeches express absolute confidence in her own opinions and contrast with Jack's utterances, quite a few of which begin hesitantly with an adverb: 'Personally...', 'Well, really...', 'Well surely...', 'Well ... may I...'. (Notice the modal verb, 'may'.) The uncertainty is not in himself but in the farcical situation. Wilde points up differences between the two in his use of stage directions. For Gwendolen: (glibly); for Jack: (nervously); (looks at her in amazement); (astounded). Notice also that Gwendolen interrupts Jack in order to get a move on: 'I would certainly advise you to do so'. In the last speech of the excerpt, Gwendolen begins in frivolous, or practical manner, whichever way you choose to take it, and ends in similar vein with a concern for social behaviour. Between these two, however, she remarks, 'What wonderfully blue eyes you have Ernest!' An actor could choose whether to make this a genuine, if momentarily, tender note, or could play it in a frivolous way. Which do you prefer?

**3** The scene, as indeed the whole play, needs to be carried off with an air of supreme confidence in verbal performance. You can hear this just by reading it aloud. The sheer certitude with which Gwendolen speaks is itself funny, while the idea of marrying somebody for the name Ernest, at first seeming absurd, is in fact a witty satire on well-to-do marriages of the day. Socially accepted families and titles were of the utmost importance. Lots of phrases have an authorial twinkle in them:

'the provincial pulpits'
'the more expensive monthly magazines'
'Besides, Jack is a notorious domesticity' (ie, a well-known nick-name)
'Men often propose for practice'.

While appearing frivolous sometime, there is also an educated, intelligent voice in Gwendolen's remarks, necessary for any kind of wit: 'Ah! That is clearly a metaphysical speculation'. Well-cultivated English accents are also necessary for relishing the full flavour of Wilde's wit.

4 In her opening remark, Gwendolen shows acute pragmatic awareness: 'Whenever people talk about the weather, I always feel quite certain that they mean something else.' Jack picks this up straightaway: 'I do mean something else'. It is interesting that as with *Romeo and Juliet*, there is an initial preoccupation with the difficulty of communicating through speech. Romeo specifically wants to make a vow, while Gwendolen wants a specific proposal from Jack. In both scenes, there is a sense of negotiation and argument. In other respects, however, many readers will find the two scenes very different so far as language is concerned. One is all poetry and trembling excitement, the other prose and self-possessed wit. One all heart, the other all head. There is an explicit, matter-of-factness in what Gwendolen and Jack say, whereas nearly everything Romeo and Juliet say has overtones and nuances of meaning, yet there is some hard-headedness in *Romeo and Juliet* while *The Importance of Being Earnest* is not entirely heartless.

It would be perfectly possible for the same pair of actors to play both couples. To appreciate the differences, make a list of the purely linguistic challenges they would have to meet in preparing their roles.

You should think about the following phonological and paralinguistic resources for conveying explicit and implicit meanings. Remember too that the actors have to communicate with an audience as well as each other.

accent
stress
variations in volume and pitch
gesture and facial expression
eye contact
pauses
timing
variations in pace
levels of emotional intensity

**ACTIVITY 11**

Annotate the passage for TV production. Think how you would instruct the cameras to reinforce, complement and contrast words and images. Make a decision, for example, on how to film the 'blue eyes' remark.

# Summary

In this chapter you have focused on ways in which writers use language to construct entirely imaginary people, situations, events, settings, moods and conversations which nevertheless have credibility in the imagination, as well as real emotional power. You have considered phonological, lexical and grammatical and pragmatic features that contribute to meaning and interpretation.

# 2 Literary Stylistics

In this chapter you will look more closely at concepts and methods that are useful for investigating literary texts, or to use a more exact term, verbal art. You will consider the following topics:

- reading like a writer
- the web of language that binds writers, texts and readers together
- verbal art
- genres
- a repertoire of essential stylistic concepts.

## Reading like a writer

In the previous chapter you explored a variety of texts using your intuitive abilities as a reader with some guidance on matters deserving special attention. This chapter looks more closely at literary stylistics and at the concepts and approaches available. Its main concern is to help you acquire a clear mind map of this area of linguistics so that you can make decisions for yourself about what to investigate and discuss in any given poem, playscript or work of prose fiction. There will be checklists, but checklists are not much use if fundamental concepts about the nature and functions of literature are not understood. In the end, the best checklist is your own, created out of reading experience and trying out different ideas.

All the texts in Chapter One come from what are termed today 'canonical books of English Literature'. Note that the word 'literature' has here acquired a capital 'L'. A canon is an authorised collection of writings, 'great works' if you like, that has been accumulated over several centuries of literature. It forms a basis for the National Curriculum, GCSE and GCE syllabuses and University courses in English Literature. The very idea of a canon, excluding as it does, many writers of poems, plays and novels is now an extremely controversial issue, as indicated by the excerpts on page 35 and featured in a 1997 NEAB English Literature examination, Critical Explorations.

# Canons to the left

*The Guardian* (October 1993)

## "Big daddies" of English literature are losing their place in the canon, finds Deborah Wolfson

In a report published this month which looks at the teaching of English in the new universities, Dr Tim Cook of Kingston University concludes that the old notion of a central canon of English literature is in danger of diversifying into 'a plethora of different canons', including the 'feminine and feminist canon' and the 'post-colonial canon'.

Based on a questionnaire sent to colleges of education and polytechnics prior to their 'universitification' the survey reveals that English literature is under attack on two fronts. It is losing its historical spread and may lose its common language, as single-subject degrees are replaced by modular courses, and some of the 'big daddies' of English literature – Chaucer, Spenser, Milton, Swift, Pope, Dryden and Shelley – lose their privileged status to recently canonised female writers such as Aphra Behn, Mary Shelley, Virginia Woolf and Sylvia Plath. Apart from Oxford and Cambridge, which continue to teach a core historical course, traditional universities have thrown out the conventional syllabus of compulsory core plus a widening range of options, and signed up for the new flexi-university based on the American model.

Patrick Parrinder, Professor of English at the University of Reading, believes that traditional universities will travel down a different path from the new universities. 'We are all introducing modularisation', Parrinder confirms, 'but that doesn't mean the single-subject course will disappear or that there will be a widespread abandonment of literature pre-1800.

'Cardiff is in the grip of a debate between traditionalists who want to retain compulsory courses and progressives who want to abolish them,' says Professor Catherine Belsey who teaches Shakespeare and sees no need for Shakespeare studies to remain compulsory.

*The extract below by Marilyn Butler comes from an article entitled 'Repossessing the Past: the Case for an Open Literary History'. The original version was a lecture given at Cambridge on the 10th November 1987. It was first published in written form in 1989.*

# Repossessing the Past. The Case for an Open Literary History

The impact of the canon on all our perceptions is perhaps most striking when we reflect how quickly and how totally it changed posterity's understanding of the two literary generations before its acceptance. In the age of Adam Smith, large numbers of general readers were able to buy or borrow books for the first time. The novels and poems offered to these new readers were often quotidian in their concerns, and direct, non-specialised in their vocabulary and range of allusion. Many authors were women; some of the best poets, we might now agree – like Burns and Black – came from the ranks. Nineteenth-century professionals, journalists and academics, made great writers into an officer class, and imposed restrictions on the entry of women and NCOs. The canon came to look harmonious rather than contentious; learned or polite rather than artless or common; national rather than provincial or sectarian on the one hand, or dispersed and international on the other. Literature is individualistic or pluralist; words such as 'canon' and 'heritage' impose a uniformity that had some practical advantages, especially at the outset, but was always artificial.

The Victorian canon must have been made for the 'general reader', more for consumption at home than in the classroom, since the process of canon-making clearly pre-dates the rise of English Literature as a school and university subject. By the second half of the nineteenth century, the era of mass secondary education, syllabus reform and the provision of academic school and university places for women, English literature was already so wholesome a field of study that its social utility was easy to argue for. Victorians, noted for their hardheadedness, saw the merits of a school subject that delivered the nation's traditions to pupils in an inspiring, unifying and easily digested form. On the most practical level, it provided models for using the language, most universal of all skills in advanced society; it opened the door to experience, personal and social, in the adult world. Given the large and steadily increasing numbers of women studying the subject, the supply of teachers was unlikely to run short. All these arguments still prevail, and are being rehearsed again in Britain, as a reforming government strives for an education system which will deliver, among other things, a mentally disciplined, trainable workforce.

**Top ten authors who are given priority in the new universities**

1. William Wordsworth
2. Emily Brontë
3. Charlotte Brontë
4. George Eliot
5. Charles Dickens
6. William Shakespeare
7. Jane Austen
8. James Joyce
9. Virginia Woolf
10. W B Yeats

**Top ten 20th century novelists**

1. D H Lawrence
2. James Joyce
3. Virginia Woolf
4. Henry James
5. Angela Carter
6. Toni Morrison
7. Margaret Atwood
8. Alice Walker
9. George Orwell
10. Chinua Achebe

Stylistics is not primarily concerned with the value or quality of texts but with a description and analysis of linguistic detail in the text, related to sociolinguistic issues underlying the text. It provides essential information for informed interpretation and evaluation of texts by showing how the language is at work in the text and in readers' minds. Looking at how language works is not drudgery. It is an exciting process of discovering why a poem can move you, why a joke can make you laugh out loud, why a play is gripping or why the ending of a novel is achingly sad. Think how a single linguistic feature can ruin any of these effects: a wrong word here, a failure to pause at the right moment, an unintended ambiguity.

Stylistics is another word for reading, but reading that can be both intensely appreciative and critical at the same time. 'Appreciative' does not mean going overboard with enjoyment any more than 'critical' means looking for things that are wrong. Together they mean being more alert as a reader, and being able to read in a variety of ways. Reading like a writer, for example, is one kind of reading that draws attention to details of construction and lexico-grammatical choices. You do not need to restrict literature to, for example, a novel written with the gravity and versatility of a Dickens or a Hardy. Stylistics is concerned with prose fiction of all kinds whether it qualifies for entry into the canon or not.

## ACTIVITY 12

For this activity you will have to write a short piece of fiction. Think of an exciting thriller that hasn't been written yet, but which you would enjoy reading if it had. The opening of any novel is bound to be important. It is the reader's first encounter with the writer and the first entry into the world of the text. The range of choice is very wide. Write about a hundred words that you think would be a good introduction to a thriller. Don't concern yourself with plot, just get the story off to a good start. Do not read the texts which follow until you have written your own text.

## COMMENTARY

Read through your text to see what choices you have made, what strategies you have adopted. Don't worry about the quality of your writing, look at its features. Have you written about a character? A place? An event or action? A conversation? Have you mixed some of these? How would you describe the tone or the way in which you have addressed your reader? Who is narrating the story? Were you conscious of choosing words for effect or did the words choose themselves? Now look at the following three texts each of which is the opening of a thriller. Don't compare them with yours in terms of quality. List different ways in which a novel can be started off, including your own way.

**(a)**

THE NAKED man who lay splayed out on his face beside the swimming pool might have been dead. He might have been drowned and fished out of the pool and laid out on the grass to dry while the police or the next-of-kin were summoned. Even the little pile of objects in the grass beside his head might have been his personal effects, meticulously assembled in full view so that no one should think that something had been stolen by his rescuers.

To judge by the glittering pile, this had been, or was, a rich man. It contained the typical membership badges of the rich man's club – a money clip, made of a Mexican fifty-dollar piece and holding a substantial wad of banknotes, a well-used gold Dunhill lighter, an oval gold cigarette case with the wavy ridges and discreet turquoise button that means Fabergé, and the sort of novel a rich man pulls out of the bookcase to take into the garden – *The Little Nugget* – an old P. G. Wodehouse. There was also a bulky gold wristwatch on a well-used brown crocodile strap. It was a Girard-Perregaux model designed for people who like gadgets, and it had a sweep second-hand and two little windows in the face to tell the day of the month, and the month, and the phase of the moon. The story it now told was 2.30 on June 10th with the moon three-quarters full.

A blue and green dragon-fly flashed out from among the rose bushes at the end of the garden and hovered in mid-air a few inches above the base of the man's spine. It had been attracted by the golden shimmer of the June sunshine on the ridge of fine blond hairs above the coccyx. A puff of breeze came off the sea. The tiny field of hairs bent gently. The dragon-fly darted nervously sideways and hung above the man's left shoulder, looking down. The young grass below the man's open mouth stirred. A large drop of sweat rolled down the side of the fleshy nose and dropped glittering into the grass. That was enough. The dragon-fly flashed away.

**(b)**

THE EYES behind the wide black rubber goggles were cold as flint. In the howling speed-turmoil of a BSA M20 doing seventy, they were the only quiet things in the hurtling flesh and metal. Protected by the glass of the goggles, they stared fixedly ahead from just above the centre of the handlebars, and their dark unwavering focus was that of gun muzzles. Below the goggles, the wind had got into the face through the mouth and had wrenched the lips back into a square grin that showed big tombstone teeth and strips of whitish gum. On both sides of the grin the cheeks had been blown out by the wind into pouches that fluttered slightly. To right and left of the hurtling face under the crash helmet, the black gauntlets, broken-wristed at the controls, looked like the attacking paws of a big animal.

The man was dressed in the uniform of a dispatch-rider in the Royal Corps of Signals, and his machine, painted olive green, was, with certain modification to the valves and the carburettor and the removal of some of the silencer baffles to give more speed, identical with a standard British Army machine. There was nothing in the man or his equipment to suggest that he was not what he appeared to be, except a fully loaded Luger held by a clip to the top of the petrol tank.

(c)

WITH its two fighting claws held forward like a wrestler's arms the big *pandinus* scorpion emerged with a dry rustle from the finger-sized hole under the rock.

There was a small patch of hard, flat earth outside the hole and the scorpion stood in the centre of this on the tips of its four pairs of legs, its nerves and muscles braced for a quick retreat and its senses questing for the minute vibrations which would decide its next move.

The moonlight, glittering down through the great thorn bush, threw sapphire highlights off the hard, black polish of the six-inch body and glinted palely on the moist white sting which protruded from the last segment of the tail, now curved over parallel with the scorpion's flat back.

Slowly the sting slid home into its sheath and the nerves in the poison sac at its base relaxed. The scorpion had decided. Greed had won over fear.

Twelve inches away, at the bottom of a sharp slope of sand, the small beetle was concerned only with trudging on towards better pastures than he had found under the thorn bush, and the swift rush of the scorpion down the slope gave him no time to open his wings. The beetle's legs waved in protest as the sharp claw snapped round his body, and then the sting lanced into him from over the scorpion's head and immediately he was dead.

After it had killed the beetle the scorpion stood motionless for nearly five minutes. During this time it identified the nature of its prey and again tested the ground and the air for hostile vibrations. Reassured, its fighting claw withdrew from the half-severed beetle and its two small feeding pincers reached out and into the beetle's flesh. Then for an hour, and with extreme fastidiousness, the scorpion ate its victim.

**COMMENTARY**

The opening sentence of text (a) is visually striking to say the least. The old adage, 'Hit the reader with a good opening sentence' seems to have been observed here. But notice too, the use of the modal verb 'might' which immediately creates uncertainty in the reader. Further uses of 'might' suggests that the narrator is either playing the reader along or following thoughts of his/her own. More uncertainty is created by the verb forms 'had been, or was'. The effect of statements of this kind is to raise questions. Is it an accident? Murder? Given some experience of the genre (even in TV form) the reader is prepared to assume the man is in fact alive, yet the author has chosen to present him in terms of death, police and a negative reference to theft.

The opening sentence of text (b) is equally striking visually. Notice the use of definite articles to convey hard-edged, immediate reality, and the adjective/noun combinations: 'the howling speed-turmoil', 'the hurtling flesh and metal', 'dark unwavering focus'. A number of concrete nouns contribute to the vividness of the word picture while the repetition of 'hurtling' reinforces an impression of high speed. Notice though that a simile is used at the beginning and end of what is in any case a sharply pictorialised opening paragraph: 'as cold as flint' and 'like the attacking paws of a big animal', along with 'tombstone teeth'. These convey a sense of danger and a presentiment of death. By this means, the imagined details of a simile add another dimension to the concrete description. Do the similes seem to you familiar ones or original?

In texts (a) and (b), the reader is introduced to a person who may or may not figure largely in the story, one inert, the other travelling at speed. Text (c) is about a scorpion which readers would not expect to be a character in a thriller. The narrative is explicit about the scorpion yet the effect of the writing is to convey to the reader a sense of danger: 'muscles braced for a quick retreat', 'senses questing', 'nerves', 'poison sac', 'fear'. Notice the use of fairly long sentences in building up the scene and the use of two very short ones in which the narrator interprets for us the scorpion's actions: 'The scorpion had decided'. The verb 'decided' is used intransitively here; the reader is not told what the decision is about. The following sentence suggests a motivation but we learn the actual decision by implication in the first line of the next paragraph.

At the end of texts (a) and (b), the reader will read on for answers: Is the man dead or not? Why introduce him in this way? Who is the rider and where is he/she going? (Note the phrases 'the face ... the mouth ... the cheeks', when a possessive pronoun might have been expected, leaving the question of gender open). At the end of text (b), the reader is left wondering when, where, with whom the story is likely to begin. The opening needs to be interpreted, contextualised as a lead-in or a symbol for what is to come – poisonous, predatory creatures, feeding on the unwary.

All three excerpts were in fact written by the same author, Ian Fleming, and are the openings of James Bond stories:

- *From Russia with Love* – Text (a)
- *For Your Eyes Only* – Text (b)
- *Diamonds are Forever* – Text (c).

Admittedly, Fleming is an extremely accomplished, popular writer, but you can still compare the actual language strategies you used with Fleming's strategies. Did you begin with conversation for example? Fleming has on other occasions but not in these three books. Did you create expectations? Questions in the reader's mind? What nouns and adjectives did you use to construct visual impressions? Did you introduce the main character straightaway? Fleming has on other occasions, but not here.

---

Reading like a writer does not mean that you have to write something before you read; it is a matter of registering what choices the author has made, and that you could make in your own original writing for coursework or for examination. Writing can write itself – a kind of internal gossip that gets onto paper – and you may be disappointed with it. Cliches, stereotypes and attitudes of mind are just waiting to be written. In speech this is often efficient and convenient; in writing it is a process that needs a careful watch, if you are to create the effect you really want. It helps enormously to be able to read your own and other people's writing through the eyes of a reader other than yourself. But that isn't easy.

There are many critics who would refuse Fleming's admission to the canon of English Literature on grounds of quality and cultural value. Regardless of whether this should be so, or whether indeed, a canon is worthwhile, Fleming, Dickens and Hardy are all writers of prose fiction in the English language and their work is of equal interest stylistically. Despite their difference, the works have many things in common. Notice, for example, the relish for detail and cartoonlike emphasis, with which Fleming constructs his motorcyclist and Dickens constructs Mr Venus's shop. Similarly in the scorpion passage, Fleming uses Hardy's technique of starting at a distant point and zooming in gradually.

Before turning to the repertoire of language resources available to storytellers, poets and dramatists, it will help to look at how everyday language whether thought, spoken, listened to, read or written is transformed into genres of writing.

# A web of language

The idea of language as a web that is both inside everybody's mind and outside in the world at large is a familiar one. Language is something we are all caught up in, ensnared by, supported by, connected by. Robert Graves refers to it as 'a cool web' (see his poem in Chapter Four).

At the living heart of the web is everyday, familiar language made up of all our dialects and idiolects. You can view it socially and collectively. Or you can view it personally.

Because stylistics requires you to make your own investigations and come to your own conclusions about texts (in an examination, for example), let's look first at language from a personal point of view. Think of all the language that makes up your idiolect, and all the situations and contexts in which you are idiolectally most at home. There's your voice characteristics, your regional dialect, the vocabulary you have acquired over the years and the way you think. You appreciate certain kinds of verbal humour, for example, and there will be people you find easier to talk to than others.

You have your own ways of expression, your own way of daydreaming and your own preferences in other people's uses of language. The most natural environment is informal talk with family and friends. Dialect will contribute much to your idiolect. Popular expressions describe it very well: chinwag, a good natter, a bit of a chat, putting the world to rights, a right good moan, a heart to heart. Sometimes it is trivial, lighthearted, something and nothing; at other times it touches on the deeply serious. It is full of jokes, wordplay, puns, word games, alliteration, verbal coincidences, howlers, spoonerisms, malapropisms, catchphrases, riddles, popular sayings, greetings and farewells.

This non-stop living language is predominantly interactive but it is also influenced by another stream of non-stop language on radio, TV and now on the Internet and e-mail. There are also other bits of language content: chatty letters, glimpsed adverts, magazines idly flipped through, T-shirt slogans, designer labels, notes, birthday card greetings, the wording on packaging, posters and pamphlets.

All in all, it is ideal stuff for generating stories, poems and plays. It is in fact the source of all kinds of writing and more formal kinds of talk. The diagram on page 41 represents on the left-hand side what might be called social, transactional, practical purpose uses of language, while on the right it represents artistic, literary, entertaining uses of language. Idiolect is at the centre of the diagram.

This book is primarilly concerned with what goes on in the bottom right hand corner, but notice that there are routes from every part of the web to every other part of the web. A traditional distinction between speaking/listening and reading/writing has been observed but media that combine the verbal with the visual have also been included to represent comprehensively the modern communication network in which we live. Nearly all the examples have been drawn from the likely experiences of A-Level students. From the point of view of literary stylistics, the left and

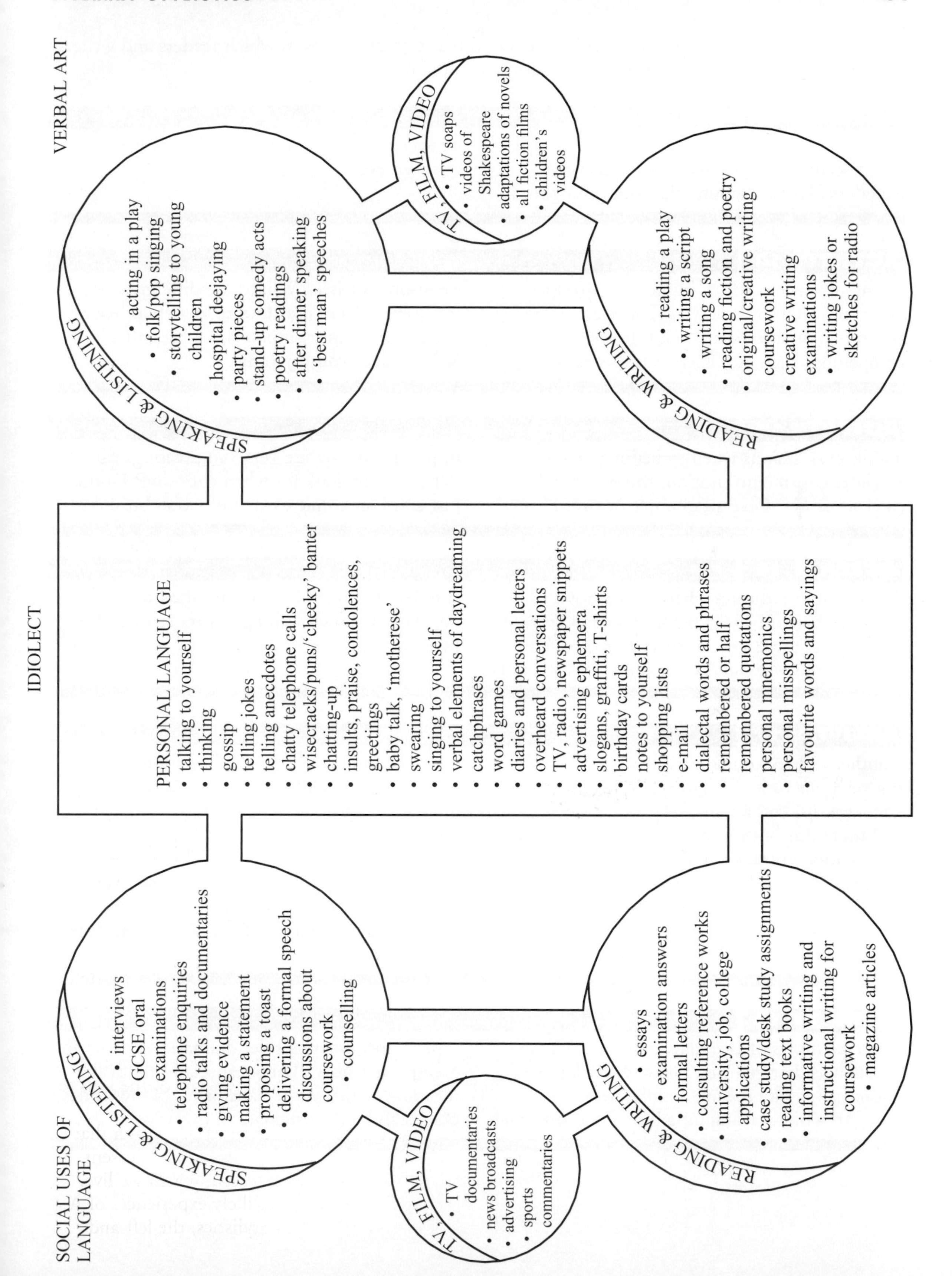
SOCIAL USES OF LANGUAGE
IDIOLECT
VERBAL ART
SPEAKING & LISTENING
• interviews
• GCSE oral examinations
• telephone enquiries
• radio talks and documentaries
• giving evidence
• making a statement
• proposing a toast
• delivering a formal speech
• discussions about coursework
• counselling
TV, FILM, VIDEO
• TV documentaries
• news broadcasts
• advertising
• sports commentaries
READING & WRITING
• essays
• examination answers
• formal letters
• consulting reference works
• university, job, college applications
• case study/desk study assignments
• reading text books
• informative writing and instructional writing for coursework
• magazine articles
PERSONAL LANGUAGE
• talking to yourself
• thinking
• gossip
• telling jokes
• telling anecdotes
• chatty telephone calls
• wisecracks/puns/'cheeky' banter
• chatting-up
• insults, praise, condolences, greetings
• baby talk, 'motherese'
• swearing
• singing to yourself
• verbal elements of daydreaming
• catchphrases
• word games
• diaries and personal letters
• overheard conversations
• TV, radio, newspaper snippets
• advertising ephemera
• slogans, graffiti, T-shirts
• birthday cards
• notes to yourself
• shopping lists
• e-mail
• dialectal words and phrases
• remembered or half remembered quotations
• personal mnemonics
• personal misspellings
• favourite words and sayings
SPEAKING & LISTENING
• acting in a play
• folk/pop singing
• storytelling to young children
• hospital deejaying
• party pieces
• stand-up comedy acts
• poetry readings
• after dinner speaking
• 'best man' speeches
TV, FILM, VIDEO
• TV soaps
• videos of Shakespeare
• adaptations of novels
• all fiction films
• children's videos
READING & WRITING
• reading a play
• writing a script
• writing a song
• reading fiction and poetry
• original/creative writing coursework
• creative writing examinations
• writing jokes or sketches for radio

right hand sides may be seen as two directions in which readers and writers may choose to go or be required to go.

**ACTIVITY 13**

Look at the central section of the diagram and note specific examples relating to your own experience. Add anything that you think should be there. Do you think your idiolect has changed ever?

**ACTIVITY 14**

Think of ways in which humour or wordplay are introduced into everyday language. Write down two or three structural features of jokes: eg openings such as, 'There was this vicar . . .'; questions, such as 'What's the difference between . . .' and plot formulae such as 'An Englishman, an Irishman and a Scotsman'. What makes you laugh most?

**ACTIVITY 15**

Think of occasions when something 'poetic' might occur in conversation, come to mind or catch your eye. Give an example or two. How important to you are verses in greetings cards? What do you look for when choosing? Don't just consider comic cards and taboo breakers.

**ACTIVITY 16**

The diagram indicates where informative, instructional and entertaining modes of writing would go if these were primary purposes, but where would you put 'persuasion'? This is not a simple question. Think of specific forms of persuasion. Much writing has more than one purpose.

**ACTIVITY 17**

Another difficult question: where would you put religious uses of language? Religious language displays a remarkable variety of forms and functions both in private and in public acts of worship. Think of examples: private prayer; a marriage rite; reading sacred scriptures; confession; preaching. A lot will depend on your religious views. Some years ago a publisher produced a version of the Bible 'designed to be read as literature'. Some readers appreciated the new layout, others objected to a fundamental error in the subtitle. The Bible they argued is a record of the acts of God, and was not designed for the purposes of literature. Think about personal, social and artistic uses of language in relation to different religious texts. Where would you put Donne's *Holy Sonnet* (see page 24)?

**ACTIVITY 18**

Select examples of everyday, personal language use such as diary entries; jokes; chatty letters; a phone call; a bad dream; an idle 'stream of thought' while waiting for a bus. Transform one into a short poem, a brief dramatic scene or an excerpt in a story. Think especially about the meaning of the word 'transform'. Many stories, poems and plays originate in this way.

**ACTIVITY 19**

Look at an example of language use on the left hand side of the diagram, for example, an interview for a job; making a police statement; the reading of a will; a school report; a genuine historical document; an accident report; a public speech.
These might be seen as extreme contrasts to artistic uses of language, but think of ways in which they might be transformed into poetry, fiction or drama. Write notes on how it might be done, making quite clear what it is that transforms fact into fiction and real-life, social activity into entertainment. Try it as a piece of coursework if you wish. Your commentary will be brimming with interesting points!

## Verbal art

Whilst there is general agreement that language functions and forms have a way of occurring in combinations and of feeding into each other, there is also general recognition of two major sets of forms and functions that can be distinguished from each other. They are exemplified by the items on each side of the diagram. What to call the two sides is a little problematical.

Traditionally, the terms 'literary' and 'non-literary' have been used but the term 'literary' is not satisfactory; it doesn't describe anything beyond saying that it is written. Moreover, there is something unsatisfactory about defining one category as a negative of the other. It inevitably puts a bias on 'literary' texts; better to define things by what they are and what they do, rather than by what they are not.

Another way of distinguishing between the two is to describe texts on the left hand side as *transactional* uses of language, and those on the right as *poetic* uses. A number of linguists (for example, Roman Jakobson and Michael Halliday) have referred to a 'poetic function' of language that produces what we call poetry and fiction. It helps to remember the Greek origins of the word: *poesis* meaning 'making' or 'a creative action'. The emphasis here is on process and effects rather than on the status of finished products. Further discussion of the term 'poetic function' and of different approaches to describing it can be found under appropriate headings in Katie Wales's *Dictionary of Stylistics* (Longman, 1989).

In *Linguistics and Literature* (Routledge, 1997), Nigel Fabb uses the term 'verbal art' as a synonym for literature but including oral as well as written, poetic texts. This is a useful term with the same meaning as 'artistic uses of language' in the diagram. Be careful though, not to confuse it with the term 'language arts', a term used in education to cover all language skills however they may be used.

The important distinction to get clear, whatever terminology you opt for, lies between language actions that take place to fulfil social and practical needs, and language actions that stem from artistic impulse. The same distinction can be observed in painting and photography. There are many practical and social uses for both, and there are many artistic forms of both ranging from the lightly decorative to the profoundly serious.

## *Wordplay*

**ACTIVITY 20**

One source of verbal art is wordplay, intended or accidental. Advertisers, slogan makers and headline writers are particularly fond of wordplay. They are, of course, putting their skill to persuasive use but play on words is also something to be enjoyed for its own sake. It may be something clever, or curious, or unusual. Collect some examples from advertising and journalism of wordplay that seem to you imaginative or clever.

# Genres

The move out of the personal, expressive zone of language (idiolect) into forms of writing is a move into genres, which are learned by both writers and readers through practical experience and critical response. A genre is an accumulation or a tradition of practices and conventions that have come to govern the way in which particular texts are written for particular purposes. There are also speech genres.

The oldest use of the term is in literary criticism to distinguish different text types: poetry, prose and drama. Poetry is then divided into sub-genres: epic, sonnet, ode, ballad, drama into tragedy and comedy and mixed genre such as tragi-comedy. Prose splits into many sub-genres: novel, short story, sermon, essay, letter, travel writing, history and so on.

But genre isn't just about labelling texts, a relatively simple stylistics activity; it is about understanding the linguistic requirements to write effectively and read appreciatively in that genre. Groups of similar texts make up a genre, and these texts in turn are language woven into shapes and patterns that construct and communicate meanings (the Latin 'texere' means 'to weave' as in 'texture').

In *Learning to Write* (Routledge, 1994), Gunther Kress writes on genre:

'Learning genres ... represents ... socialisation into appropriate and accepted modes of organising knowledge ... and into ways of representing perceptions and knowledge to others. The learning of genre is therefore intimately linked with the codification of knowledge in society, and with the modes of organising and communicating information to others. This represents a vast convenience to society and no doubt to individuals. If our modes of establishing, encoding, organising and transmitting knowledge differed markedly from individual to individual, there is no doubt that society would be quite different, and probably less efficient. However it is important to recognise, first, that the genres have this constraining effect and, second, that they are conventions. Other conventions can be imagined ...'.

**ACTIVITY 21**

Kress is suggesting that knowing how to produce an appropriate text depends upon knowing about expectations and conventions within the genre to which that text belongs ... knowing the code in fact. The excerpt is not an easy one to read first time but repays time and thought spent on it.

First re-read the excerpt two or three times, getting clear in your own mind what is meant by:

- socialisation
- organising knowledge and information
- codification
- representing
- constraining effect
- conventions.

Think of specific examples. In geography, for example, a survey report would be a way of organising knowledge; a map would exemplify representation; codification would be the use of such concept words as 'urbanisation', 'subsistence', 'yield' and 'gross national product'. Think back on your experience of schooling, focusing on a particular GCSE subject (not English).

**ACTIVITY 22**

Think about Case Study and Desk Study examinations and consider how much understanding of genres they require. Use Kress's terminology.

**ACTIVITY 23**

Poetry is a genre many people find difficult to get into. In *The Problem with Poetry* (Open University, 1991), Richard Andrews writes: 'Poetry is . . . both revealing and cryptic at the same time . . . It is seen as the most distant from "everyday life", as the least "useful" of the arts, as inhabiting an enclosed, self-reverential world to which only an elite gain access.' How far do you agree with this? What is your explanation of 'the problem'? If you like poetry, explain how to get into the genre as a reader. Choose a favourite poem to illustrate your approach to poetry.

**ACTIVITY 24**

There is a huge range of popular fiction on the market today. Best selling paperbacks have print runs of millions of copies. See how many sub-genres of popular fiction you can think of and give at least one example for each eg: Hollywood scandals; war stories; Mills and Boon romances; horror stories; fantasy adventures.

## *Genre and stylistics*

If genres are readers' and writers' conventions, what then are the expectations that stylistics has to take into account when exploring verbal art, or literary texts?

### Prose fiction

Some of the following features seem essential to the prose fiction genre, others are very common:

- entering an imagined world that is nevertheless 'believable'
- some 'imitation' of reality

- content consisting of setting, events, characters, conversation, thoughts, a plot or storyline
- a narrative voice (a storyteller)
- cultural themes such as love, death, money, crime, fate
- emotional content (with intellectual balance)
- a sense of an ending
- orientation of the reader in relation to fictional content
- a time scale of some kind
- pleasure in formal construction
- implicit as well as explicit meanings (symbols, imagery)
- some obscurity or 'difficulty' in meaning
- cohesion and consistency
- experimentation with conventions of fiction
- 'atmosphere'
- a poetic dimension.

## Verse

Some of the following are characteristic of verse, others are very common:

- unusual word choice and sentence construction so that the language draws attention to itself
- short, or shortish, texts compared with prose fiction
- noticeable features of metre, stress and rhythm
- cultural themes such as love, nature, 'life'
- phonological features
- metaphor and imagery
- meaning not immediately accessible
- distinct formal construction
- distinct text layout on the page
- emotional content.

## Drama

Some essential and very common features of drama are:

- requires actors and use of speaking voice
- two audiences, one on stage, one in auditorium
- imitates natural speech to greater or less extent
- language accompanied by real action
- distinct formal construction of Acts and scenes
- physical context of stage or studio
- authorial voice in stage directions.

**ACTIVITY 25**

Look again at the excerpts you have explored so far: Dickens, Hardy, Fleming, Shelley, Donne, Wordsworth, Shakespeare, Wilde. Which aspects of genre conventions do you find in each excerpt? Are there any aspects not listed here? Remember, you are looking at genre conventions, not at stylistic features of individual texts, which is the final topic of this chapter.

# A stylistics repertoire

The notion of a repertoire applied to language is a useful one. Everybody has an idiolectal repertoire of words and phrases, ways of talking to people and ways of thinking about everyday things. Once you move into a writing genre, modifications and additions have to be made to idiolect to incorporate language from the genre repertoire and to produce a text that fits in with genre conventions and expectations. Stylistics requires some knowledge of that language repertoire.

There are, of course, general linguistic items in the repertoire which you need to be aware of whenever you are reading critically and whatever kind of text you are reading. In an examination answer, you may choose not to highlight or even mention some of them, but they should always be in the back of your mind. The following are all part of the stylistics stock in trade:

- pronouns
- abstract/concrete nouns
- double/triple adjectives
- use of adverbials
- tense choices
- modal verbs
- use of active/passive
- sentence length
- structure and function
- semantic fields
- lexical choice
- figures of speech
- punctuation.

One of the constant problems for students learning about stylistics is bridging the gap between big issues of genre, audience, purpose, sociolinguistic context and little details of language in use at word and sentence level. Many weak answers in examinations get lost in generalisations that are never pinned down to evidence in the text, or are lost in pointless observations ('The writer uses concrete nouns' or 'there is a modal verb in the second sentence') the significance of which eludes both the candidate and the examiner.

You are now going to consider some concepts that will help you make connections between the big, interpretative ideas about a literary text and the descriptive, nitty-gritty of linguistic observation. The terms used are not meant as a checklist, since not all features will be relevant to every text you read. However, this is the repertoire you need to rummage in to find appropriate focal points for your explorations.

## *Action*

A useful concept not only to distinguish verbs (dynamic/stative) but also the movement of a narrative from one event to another.

Dramatic action can be in the dialogue, and the word is also used to mean plot. The writer actioned the text in the first place and the reader re-activates it every time it is read. Compare the different kinds of action in the Dickens, Hardy and Fleming excerpts. Remember that writing about action in fiction is a choice; there are many other things to write about at any point in a novel or short story.

## *Addresser/addressee*

A sense of these is always important. Authors do not necessarily address readers directly. They can address themselves or characters in the story as well as choosing to address the reader. The term 'implied reader' is useful for referring to the addressee who seems to be assumed. How does Fleming address his readers? Is the reader addressed from a different standpoint in *Ozymandias* than in Donne's *Holy Sonnet*? Could it be, in the latter, that the addressee is not a person at all? Poetry often addresses non-persons like trees, the sun, a bird.

## *Adjacency pairs*

A familiar enough term used in the analysis of spontaneous conversations, but think of the artistic control a writer has over who says what. Pay particular attention to the crafting of dialogue in novels and plays. Notice that the witty ripostes of a Wilde play often occur as paired remarks, one capping the other. Look also beyond pairs, at interchanges which seem sculpted to particular effects. You could compare the scene in *Romeo and Juliet* with a love scene from another Shakespeare play.

## *Alienation*

In one sense, the term describes the distance readers tend to put between the 'baddies' and themselves. The term 'identification' similarly describes the closeness readers feel with 'goodies'. With many of Shakespeare's characters, it is possible to veer between alienation and identification.

For Bertolt Brecht, alienation was a political issue to keep ideologies and propaganda at bay; in stylistics, you need to rise above the feelings generated by effective writing, in order to describe just what effects are being created and how? Look at the two Dickens excerpts and measure your alienation/identification ratings. Remember, and this is the key issue, the characters were all constructed in the author's imagination and are re-constructed in the reader's. Always bear in mind that the writer has *chosen* to portray a character in a certain way. What you read is a reflection of what appeals to the writer or of how the writer views character.

What makes the third Fleming excerpt significantly different from the other novel excerpts? You may feel that he is using a deliberately alienating device to introduce dangerous people.

## *Ambiguity*

Ambiguity seems central to literature, especially poetry. Yet ambiguity occurs often enough in everyday life; it is context that often makes the meaning clear. All over the country there are notices giving the impression that the law is in pursuit of a man called Bill Posters. The context, of course, makes clear that people who put up advertising notices without permission will be prosecuted. Ambiguity in poetry, by accident or design, adds dimensions of meaning. It can be comic in *Alice in Wonderland*:

'How is bread made?'
'I know that!' Alice cried eagerly. You take some flour –'
'Where do you pick the flower?' the White Queen asked. 'In a garden or in the hedges?'
'Well, it is not picked at all,' Alice explained: 'it's ground –'
'How many acres of ground?' said the White Queen.

It can have tragic implications in *Romeo and Juliet.* Look at the ambiguous replies Juliet gives her mother in Act Three, scene five. Do you detect any ambiguity in the scene with Romeo explored earlier?

E. O. Parrott in *How to be Well-Versed in Poetry* (Viking, 1990) describes ambiguity as 'A convenient domain for the poet to retreat when he is not sure of his own meaning.' The truth of the matter is that so many English words are polysemic (have more than one meaning) ambiguities are lurking everywhere in both readers' and writers' minds.

## *Anticipation*

A mixture of expecting, guessing and suspense generated in readers' minds by features in the text. The student who began a story as follows, knew exactly what she was doing:

I never thought I'd see the day when I was glad to be walking up the school drive in good time for registration.

As did Dickens when he began *David Copperfield*:

Whether I shall turn out to be the hero of my own life, or whether that station will be held by anybody else, these pages must show.

Readers are constantly anticipating; sometimes their anticipations are confirmed, sometimes surprised.

## *Antonymy*

The contrasting of individual words and semantic fields with opposite meanings occurs frequently in literature but also in other genres such as politics, advertising and all kinds of persuasive writing. Remember to look out for them as you scan the lexis of a text; don't forget them! Sometimes the contrasts are not exactly opposite as in Tolstoy's *War and Peace* but interestingly different as in Jane Austen's *Pride and Prejudice* and *Sense and Sensibility.*

## *Asides*

Asides have very interesting effects in a play depending on how naturalistic the play's style is. In a naturalistic play, an aside would in fact break the illusion by addressing the audience directly. Try inserting one into the Wilde excerpt and see what happens. In Shakespeare's plays, asides are frequent and a convention of the day.

## *Assonance*

Alliteration is the sound feature in texts most readily recognised, though frequently too much is made of it. In a language of about half a million words and only twenty-four consonant phonemes, it is not surprising that accidental alliterations occur all the time. Assonance, on the other hand is comparatively neglected by A-Level English Language students, yet it contributes a great deal to the sound effect of a line of poetry. Whereas alliteration is a recurring initial consonant sound, assonance is a recurring vowel sound. 'She met her fate in the lake' is an example of assonance; 'He threw the fake in the lake' is assonance that also rhymes.

## *Audience*

This is a common enough word in linguistics, rightly so. In the context of literature it often means 'reading public'. When discussing responses to texts and the effects of stylistic features remember that, whilst you are a representative of that reading public, trying to be objective, you are relying on your own reading. In stylistics, the term 'reader' is better focused than the more general term 'audience'.

## *Character*

Characters in literature vary from the remarkably vivid (Tess, Bradley Headstone, Silas Wegg) to those who are little more than a name remembered with difficulty. It is not surprising that the vivid ones seduce us into believing they really exist. It is important, for this reason, to remember that they are the constructs of authors. Often too they are as much reflections of contemporary social types as they are individual creations.

Stereotypes fit popular conceptions; there is nothing wrong with this kind of characterisation so long as you recognise it. Many writers struggle to keep stereotypes at bay, much more concerned with catching a little bit of true character from 'real life'. This is worth remembering when writing an original story or biography for coursework. Stereotypes have a way of creeping into the imagination and writers themselves if you are not careful.

## *Closure*

This is a modern, specialist term which refers to the degree of closedness or open-endedness a novel or a poem displays. If for example, a story had no ending, the reader may well feel cheated or may choose to make his own ending. Plots and storylines can be regarded as devices that close a novel by eliminating possibilities. Poems on the other hand can often seem completely open and difficult, until someone comes along and closes the poem by explaining its meaning. Non-literary texts such as newspaper stories and TV documentaries are frequently criticised for being closed, that is they permit only one interpretation and reflect one ideology. Jacques Derrida, famous for deconstructing texts to get at the ideology behind them, nevertheless had a great respect and passion for literature (see *Acts of Literature,* edited by Derek Attridge, Routledge, 1992). For him, literary texts were completely lacking in closure, permitting many interpretations. Certainly, it is in literature that a reader will find linguistic experimentation.

Finally, closure is a practical problem for A-Level English Literature examiners and writers of text books. When composing a set of texts for a Case Study type examination, or selecting prose fiction excerpts, it is an extremely difficult business to know where to end an excerpt. This is literally an act of closure and debate often ensues about the start and the cut-off point. You could experiment by setting yourself a limit of about one hundred words and then searching in a novel for one or two excerpts that could stand alone. In examinations, always ask yourself what makes the opening and closing points of an excerpt particularly apt.

## *Codes and codification*

Some ideas relevant to stylistics come from a French critic, Roland Barthes (*S/Z*, translated and published in English, Jonathan Cape, 1975). He describes five ways in which the flux of real life experiences are codified in novels and short stories. Codes (eg the rags to riches theme) give meaning to what would otherwise be a series of happenings. They are not codes in a secret sense so much as constructs and patterns of behaviour. Readers, he says, in making sense of what they are reading, attend to one or some or all of the following:

- sequence of action
- the problems and solutions ('mysteres') in the narrative (see also work of Labov and Hoey)
- characterisation
- thematic developments and oppositions (symbolic elements)
- references to culture and historical period outside the text.

Try out each of these by looking at the Dickens and Hardy excerpts again. True, you have only excerpts to go on so a little bit of skim reading (to get a plot summary) will be necessary for the first of these, though you should be able to make some deductions about the fifth from the excerpts alone.

## *Collocation*

Always be alert, particularly in poetry, for unexpected or unusual collocations, for example, 'bats with baby faces' (T. S. Eliot). Much of everyday language is made up of habitual collocations and clichés. This is not to be deplored though. One of the pleasures of poetry, and sometimes of storytelling, is the surprise effect of unusual adjective/noun pairs, eg 'blue skies green fields'.

## *Connotations*

Poets, storytellers and advertisers all know the value of connotations. Indeed, it is sometimes necessary to avoid words because their connotations will trigger unwanted reactions. The term covers all kinds of associations but in stylistics, be careful not to chase personal connotations; try to keep in touch with what you feel is a corpus of word associations readily understood by most people. When reading texts from an earlier period you need to be aware that connotations change like any other aspect of language. Find one or two words in the Dickens and Hardy excerpts and in the poems that you think would have generated different connotations at different times.

## Construct

Language enables poets, playwrights and novelists to create complete fictions. 'If you didn't have language you wouldn't be able to tell lies', said one ten-year-old girl, summarising the whole of literature in one sentence. The constructs may mirror life with extraordinary truth (verisimilitude) or they may imaginatively illuminate life with fantasy, humour or profound significance. They remain, however, constructs. According to the publicity offices of all the British and Australian soap operas, letters are regularly received from viewers who appear to believe in the real life existence of the events and characters. Don't give that impression on your A-Level Language or Literature papers!

## Defamiliarisation

In the early 1900s, significant contributions to our understanding of the processes of reading and writing poetry and fiction were made by Russian thinkers, and by what has become known as the Prague School. Both groups were interested in the ways in which literary writing de-familiarises language. By various means (devices) in the repertoire, writers surprise, even shock, readers into seeing things differently by using language in unconventional ways. Blake's *The Tyger* is often cited as an example that changes the way people think about tigers. Accumulations of conventional meanings can get in the way of saying something new or fresh. Gerard Manley Hopkins is famous for the radical ways in which his poetry makes readers see things anew, while the prose of James Joyce can still surprise and even baffle. The Beatles too, broke a language mould with the phrase *A Hard Day's Night*.

The terms 'deviance' and 'foregrounding' are used in connection with de-familiarisation (see below).

## Deviance

This is an unfortunate term if thought of in sociological, pathological or criminal terms. By 'deviance', the Prague School writers meant that literary uses of language, verbal art, deviate from everyday norms of language use. Choose any one of the texts explored so far and re-write according to the norms of ordinary language. The historical difference between now and then will only serve to illustrate the point. You could choose a Fleming excerpt and still find examples of language use that deviate from everyday norms. When did you last speak a sentence of the kind that opens *Diamonds are Forever*? Do people ever talk like a book?

## *Dialect*

In varying degrees, novelists and dramatists attempt to convey regional dialect features – lexis, pronunciation, grammar. There is always a danger of stereotyping, especially in novels where there are no actors to speak or imitate a dialect. Compromises also have to be made between representing authentic speech and making it comprehensible to readers. The term 'eye-dialect' describes the use of phonetic spelling to give the reader an indication of how the speech would sound. An example is 'theseyer cakes' spoken by Mrs Hogget in *The Sheep-Pig* (see page 62).

## *Foregrounding*

This is a term introduced into the stylistics repertoire by the Prague School originally. It has a similar meaning to 'defamiliarisation' and refers to artistically motivated deviations and patternings of the everyday language repertoire. Repetitions, alliteration, unusual figures of speech, parallelisms are all examples of foregrounding a linguistic feature for special effect. Even metre, insofar as it is more regularly patterned than everyday speech, is an example of foregrounding. Again, advertisers and comedians also know about foregrounding. It draws special attention to, for example, a rhyming pattern, a pun, an ambiguity, and highlights it.

## *Form*

A much used word in linguistic contexts, 'form' may be thought of as an essential element in artistic, literary uses of language. Texts in a particular genre may take different forms. Poetry, for example displays a variety of regular forms, such as the sonnet, as well as many experimental forms both within the structure of the poem and in the visual layout on the page.

Form, linguistically speaking, isn't just a matter of fitting the content into an appropriate overall structure, it is a matter of matching the style of expression (eg degree of formality) to the content.

## *Frame*

When you are watching a film or play on TV that has already started, it can be annoying when somebody joins you and keeps asking questions. What they want is the frame so that they do not feel disoriented and can begin to make sense of what is going on. This need for a frame, and the beginning of a novel for example is a key framing device, is a principle reason why excerpts can be difficult to work on, stylistically. The frame, given as far as possible as an introductory statement to an exam question, provides contextual support to the meaning of individual sections of a narrative.

The term originated in art criticism and is also used in media studies. It is interesting, for example, to observe what a difference 'cropping' can make to a photograph (deciding how much to cut off the four sides to reduce and 'frame' a larger picture).

'Breaking frame' is a term used to describe such things as asides and epilogues in Elizabethan or Brechtian plays, or to describe what happens when a TV actor or comedian steps outside the script and speaks directly to the camera. Prologues are usually frame makers since they introduce what is to come. Frankie Howerd's *Up Pompeii* sketches were famous for their 'prologues', with Howerd playing both narrator and a principal character. Sponsors of TV programmes also frame episodes of *Coronation Street* sponsored by Cadburys and *Heartbeat* framed by Yorkshire Tea.

## *Gap*

This means literally a break in a narrative, for example, between chapters or to convey shift in time scale. It also refers to all the things a narrator need not tell the readers because they can supply it themselves. There is no need to overkill description for example, when readers are quite capable of filling in the gaps. The term 'et cetera principle' is sometimes used. There is a very significant gap of time between the two halves of Shakespeare's *A Winter's Tale*. In silent films a well known gap filler is the insertion of a phrase such as 'Two years later'. In *The Sheep Pig*, which you will be exploring in the next chapter, there is a remarkable gap before the ending of the first chapter.

## *Grice's maxims*

Grice's philosophical maxims of quantity, quality, relevance and manner are fairly familiar to A-Level students applying them to conversational analysis. They seem very much common sense things to say about the ways in which we talk to each other. Generally speaking they are maxims of sufficiency: don't speak too long; be truthful; keep to the point; and don't be ambiguous or obscure, and don't exaggerate. Notice how, in literature, every one of these maxims is broken frequently, deliberately and enjoyably.

## *Imagery*

Imagery in literature is not used for decoration; it is used to defamiliarise language or to foreground a meaning that may not easily be apparent in literal expression. It throws a new light on the familiar or the unnoticed. Look at some of the imagery in the poems and prose fiction you have explored already, select one or two examples and explain the extra dimension of meaning provided. Little has been said of semantics so far, but an important aspect of literary stylistics is showing how literal and figurative meanings contribute to the interpretation of texts.

## *Narrator and narrative*

In the structure of writing/reading, narrators are powerful people and the narrative is a powerful vehicle driven by the narrator. Once underway, a good narrative makes the reader want to know how it will end. In *The Cambridge Encyclopedia of Language*, David Crystal identifies five ways of telling a story (see page 78 of the encyclopedia). Look at his examples and decide which kind the Dickens, Hardy and Fleming narratives are. Because the narrator is important as a framer of events, by implicit or explicit commentary, it is important in stylistics to get a clear idea of the role of the narrator and the type of narrative you are reading.

## *Metaphor*

It is easy to limit an understanding of the power of metaphor by thinking of it as a device located at a particular point in a text. Sometimes it is, but once introduced it can have a pervasive effect on the whole text. In *Ozymandias* the 'hand' metaphorically 'mocked', yet the broken statue is itself a mockery and the whole poem may be taken as a metaphor for the vanity of earthly rulers. Similarly Wegg's shop is a metaphor for dead things in the past that pervade the lives of the living characters in *Our Mutual Friend.* Don't overplay the use of metaphor, but don't neglect it either.

## *Parallelism*

Strictly speaking the word refers to exact lexical, phonological or grammatical parallels. 'Veni, vidi, vici', in its Latin form is an example of alliterative parallelism, grammatical parallelism and very near parallelism in assonance. In the English translation 'I came, I saw, I conquered' there is pronoun parallelism and the grammatical parallelism of three simple SV sentences in a row. Any evidence of balancing of sound, lexis, meaning, rhythm or grammatical structure can be regarded as parallelism.

## *Paraphrase*

It is generally considered that poetry is unparaphrasable. The moment you put its 'meaning' into prose, the poetry flies out of the window. Try paraphrasing into modern English three or four lines of a poem and examine what has been lost, and if anything has been gained. Gains in denotative meaning, for example, may be at the expense of connotative meaning.

## *Performance*

The term 'performance' is well established in linguistics as a term signifying variations in the use of a common language. Competence is the total range of possibilities within the language. Performance is what individuals do with it. In literary stylistics, as indeed in all kinds of verbal art, there is another meaning to performance, especially relevant to drama. Drama are written for two audiences. The immediate readers are the actors, presenters and directors who perform the text for another audience. Romeo and Juliet, and Gwendolen and Jack, are not just talking to each other, they are performing before an audience. It is important to have this awareness when exploring a drama excerpt otherwise you will think of it only as a text on the page and in your head. You will need to hear the text and see the accompanying action in your imagination. Echo phonology, imagining the talk (and the pauses and the timing), needs to be heard by an inner ear.

## *Readerly*

This is an English translation of the French 'lisible' used by the critic Roland Barthes. Readerly texts are classic texts that are relatively easy to read because they belong to a familiar tradition. Barthes' view is that they can be read or consumed quite passively. In contrast there are texts that are 'scriptible', that is to say 'writerly' texts. These are more difficult, more challenging, and tend to be very up to date. They require much more effort and participation from the reader.

## *Reader response and text reception*

In the 19th century, critical approaches to texts tended to focus on the writer as the inspired, personal creator of the text or as inspired person through whom the muses spoke. In the early part of the 20th century (especially the 1920s) there was a shift away from the inspired author (now dead and gone) to the surviving text in its own right. The New Critics, as they came to be called, argued that the text alone was what mattered, knowledge of writers and their times being quite irrelevant. Marxist, Psychoanalytical and Feminist critics have of course always denied this, insisting on the importance of social and historical contexts. However, over the past 40 years or so, attention has shifted yet again, this time onto the reader as a maker of meanings in texts; hence the term 'reader response'. Reception theory, derived from the work of German scholars in the 1960s, emphasises the importance of readers' knowledge, cultural experience and expectations for the reception of new texts. *Trainspotting* is a good example with which to consider how readers receive new texts and how they are absorbed into contemporary reading culture.

Reception theorists are also interested in intertextuality though the term was first introduced by the French linguist, Julia Kristeva, in the 1960s (see bibliography). Essentially the term refers to the way texts appear in other texts by direct reference, echo, allusion, and all kinds of intended and unintended other means. The more widely read you are in a culture, and that includes songs, adverts, and images, not just books, the more you will notice the ways in which texts feed off each other. You will also have a richer context in which to receive, understand and enjoy new texts. Again, advertisers know only too well the advantages of echoing other texts. Shakespeare, for example, regularly crops up in texts of all kinds eg cigars (*Hamlet*); telephones (*Romeo and Juliet*).

## *Speech*

However stylised and formal a literary text may be, there will nevertheless be a connection somewhere with the spoken voice. In an obvious but still essential way, plays are all talk, but it is also important in stylistics to be able to hear the voice, or voices, in prose fiction and poetry.

Direct speech is important in fiction because it is more expressive than indirect speech. It conveys character, allows for exclamations, interjections and terms of address which will in turn reveal emotions, relationships, dialect and attitude: luvvy, ey up mi duck, our kid, my good woman, darling, chuck, sir.

Direct speech foregrounds the utterance; notice how popular verbatim reports and headlines are in newspapers. The term 'free direct speech' can be used to refer to direct speech which is free standing and not framed by phrases such as '... he said' or 'She called out ...'. Free direct speech in an otherwise cohesive narrative leaves the reader in no doubt as to who said what but it dispenses with an intrusive narrator. There is also 'free indirect speech' that usually brings the narrator and a character together as though the narrator has slipped into a character's mind. Dickens uses it in *Hard Times* significantly with one of his most awkwardly created, tragic characters: Stephen Blackpool. The character is visiting a ruthless industrialist and villain of the piece, Mr Bounderby:

> Mr Bounderby was at his lunch. So Stephen was expected. Would the servant say that one of the Hands begged leave to speak to him?

Compare this with the way speech is handled in the two excerpts from *Our Mutual Friend.*

## *Thought*

Literary stylistics pays attention not only to ways in which speech is presented in texts but also to the ways in which the narrator's and the characters' thoughts are presented. Direct thought can be tagged by such phrases as 'she thought', 'he wondered', 'she mused', 'he said to himself'. Free direct thought dispenses with the tags and also the speech marks. It is characteristic of interior monologues and usually has a direct appeal to the reader. It can be dramatic, reflective, hesitant, decisive, and is also effective for expressing mixed feelings.

Free indirect thought similarly dispenses with tag clauses reporting thought and is used in stream of consciousness narratives. Dickens uses it in *David Copperfield* to convey Copperfield's recollections of his early life. Look at the opening pages. Compare it with the opening of *Great Expectations.*

## *Voice*

The notion of 'voice' is very important for stylistic analysis and is the one that examination candidates frequently do not recognise or describe adequately. Aspects of voice have already been considered under the heading of speech. Voice here is not just what the characters are made to say to each other in plays and novels, it is how the writer's voice comes through to the reader. A term that has traditionally been used by literary critics is 'tone' but 'voice' is more specific.

Read the opening sections of *Sons and Lovers* by D. H. Lawrence and *Passage To India* by E. M. Forster, where you will detect two very different voices. Then read Richard Hoggart's essay in a collection significantly called, *Speaking To Each Other,* in which he reflects on the voices of the two novelists as expressed in these opening passages.

It is essential that you put into words how you think you are being addressed in a poem or a novel, and indeed, by the voice of the playwright behind the characters' speeches. There is a distinct Oscar Wilde voice behind the excerpt from *The Importance of Being Earnest.*

One modern scholar who has given thought to the authorial voice that speaks to readers is the Russian, Mikhail Bakhtin (1895–1975). For him, the novel represents the most completely human of communications, expressing all the complexity and heterogeneity of men and women. In a novel, writers engage in a dialogue with readers but it is not just a one-to-one, it is a multifaceted, social dialogue involving all the readers who have shared and enjoyed, or been puzzled and intrigued by the novel. The idea of a dialogue between storyteller and reader/listener can also be applied to poetry.

Do remember that texts are not simply one dialogue between a writer and a reader. There are different voices speaking in a poem like *Ozymandias*, for example. Look also at the first part of Eliot's *The Waste Land*, and count the number of voices you can hear.

Writers often allow different voices to speak through them and are sometimes possessed by a voice. They frequently adopt a voice, rather like playing a role. What sort of literary voice do you detect in the Fleming excerpts? How do the poetic voices of Donne, Shelley and Wordsworth differ? How might Oscar Wilde have 'told' the Romeo and Juliet story, or is that an impossible idea?

In the next three chapters you will have an opportunity to apply these ideas to texts drawn from prose fiction, poetry and drama.

## Summary

In this chapter you have concentrated on the language resources available to imaginative and creative writers. You have also considered some essential ideas that will help you to go beyond the merely feature-spotting approach to stylistics, and begin to explore more subtly your reading experience, together with the many factors that go into the creation of verbal art in prose and verse. Texts assign readers a role to play just as the characters in a play or a story have their roles.

# 3 The Art of the Storyteller

## Survey

In this chapter you will explore examples of prose fiction including a children's story, thrillers and a short story by Katherine Mansfield. Activities will focus on:

- *The Sheep-Pig* by Dick King-Smith, an excellent example of the storyteller's art
- *Miss Brill* by Katherine Mansfield, a perfectly crafted short story
- The sense of an ending: a look at how stories end.

You will look in considerable detail at the ways in which the authors make their lexical and grammatical choices as they weave their narratives, and at how the reader's imagination responds to the story being told.

## Writing for young readers

One of the very enjoyable aspects of modern linguistic approaches to literary texts is the exploration of story structures, especially in fairy stories, folk tales and nursery tales. The Russian formalist critics, aptly named because of their interest in the forms such narratives take, have contributed a great deal. If you would like to know more, as background for a project for example, read Tzvetan Todorov's *Introduction to Poetics* (Harvester, 1981). The term 'poetics' is used here in the sense of 'making' or 'constructing' and refers to prose narratives as well as poetry.

It is quite surprising to discover how many different versions of *Cinderella* and *Sleeping Beauty* there are across European literatures. It is also fascinating to explore the way in which 'threes' occur in many nursery tales: *The Three Little Pigs*; *The Three Billy Goats Gruff*; *Goldilocks and the Three Bears.*

In the first activity you are going to explore, not a fairy story, but a modern story written for children by Dick King-Smith, *The Sheep-Pig.* The excerpt is in fact the complete first chapter, so you will also have an opportunity to read for real as it were, instead of studying a disembodied excerpt. In addition you will be able to study closely the arts and crafts of writing for chidren, a popular genre for original writing coursework, the demands of which are often underestimated.

## *The Sheep-Pig by Dick King-Smith*

**ACTIVITY 26**

Read the opening chapter of *The Sheep-Pig*. Make sure you hear it as well as look at the print. Then go through the text writing down everything you notice about the language and the way the narrative unfolds. See if some of the ideas listed at the end of the last chapter help you to see more of what is going on in the text.

# Chapter I

### "Guess my weight"

"What's that noise?" said Mrs Hogget, sticking her comfortable round red face out of the kitchen window. "Listen, there 'tis again, did you hear it, what a racket, what a row, anybody'd think someone was being murdered, oh dearie me, whatever is it, just listen to it, will you?"

Farmer Hogget listened. From the usually quiet valley below the farm came a medley of sounds: the oompah oompah of a brass band, the shouts of children, the rattle and thump of a skittle alley, and every now and then a very high, very loud, very angry-sounding squealing lasting perhaps ten seconds.

Farmer Hogget pulled out an old pocket-watch as big round as a saucer and looked at it. "Fair starts at two," he said. "It's started."

"I knows that," said Mrs Hogget, "because I'm late now with all theseyer cakes and jams and pickles and preserves as is meant to be on the Produce Stall this very minute, and who's going to take them there, I'd like to know, why you are, but afore you does, what's that noise?"

The squealing sounded again.

"That noise?"

Mrs Hogget nodded a great many times. Everything that she did was done at great length, whether it was speaking or simply nodding her head. Farmer Hogget, on the other hand, never wasted his energies or his words.

"Pig," he said.

Mrs Hogget nodded a lot more.

"I thought 'twas a pig, I said to meself that's a pig that is, only nobody round here do keep pigs, 'tis all sheep for miles about, what's a pig doing, I said to meself, anybody'd think they was killing the poor thing, have a look when you take all this stuff down, which you better do now, come and give us a hand, it can go in the back of the Land Rover, 'tisn't raining, 'twon't hurt, wipe your boots afore you comes in."

"Yes," said Farmer Hogget.

When he had driven down to the village and made his delivery to the Produce Stall, Farmer Hogget walked across the green, past the Hoopla Stall and the Coconut Shy and the Aunt Sally and the skittles and the band, to the source of the squealing noise, which came every now and again from a small pen of hurdles in a far corner, against the churchyard wall.

By the pen sat the Vicar, notebook in hand, a cardboard box on the bale in front of him. On the hurdles hung a notice – "Guess my weight. Ten pence a go." Inside was a little pig.

As Farmer Hogget watched a man leaned over and picked it out of the pen. He hefted it in both hands, frowning and pursing his lips in a considering way, while all the time the piglet struggled madly and yelled blue murder. The moment it was put down, it quietened. Its eyes, bright intelligent eyes, met the farmer's. They regarded one another.

One saw a tall thin brown-faced man with very long legs, and the other saw a small fat pinky-white animal with very short ones.

"Ah, come along, Mr Hogget!" said the vicar. "You never know, he could be yours for ten pence. Guess his weight correctly, and at the end of the day you could be taking him home!"

"Don't keep pigs," said Farmer Hogget. He stretched out a long arm and scratched its back. Gently, he picked it up and held it before his face. It stayed quite still and made no sound.

"That's funny," said the Vicar. "Every time so far that someone has picked him up he's screamed his head off. He seems to like you. You'll have to have a guess."

Carefully, Farmer Hogget put the piglet back in the pen. Carefully, he took a ten pence from his pocket and dropped it in the cardboard box. Carefully, he ran one finger down the list of guesses already in the Vicar's note-book.

"Quite a variation," said the Vicar. "Anything from twenty pounds to forty, so far." He wrote down 'Mr Hogget' and waited, pencil poised.

Once again, slowly, thoughtfully, the farmer picked the piglet up.

Once again, it remained still and silent.

"Thirty-one pounds," said Farmer Hogget. He put the little pig down again. "And a quarter," he said.

"Thirty-one and a quarter pounds. Thank you, Mr Hogget. We shall be weighing the little chap at about half past four."

"Be gone by then."

"Ah well, we can always telephone you. If you should be lucky enough to win him."

"Never win nothing."

As he walked back across the green, the sound of the pig's yelling rang out as someone else had a go.

"You do never win nothing," said Mrs Hogget at tea-time, when her husband, in a very few words, had explained matters, "though I've often thought I'd like a pig, we could feed 'un on scraps, he'd come just right for Christmas time, just think, two nice hams, two sides of bacon, pork chops, kidneys, liver, chitterling, trotters, save his blood for black pudding, there's the phone."

Farmer Hogget picked it up.

"Oh," he said.

**COMMENTARY**

There follows a running commentary on the first chapter of *The Sheep-Pig*.

The title of the book immediately foregrounds something out of the ordinary – not a sheepdog but a sheep-pig! What is to be expected? Some readers may have seen the film version, *Babe*, which is a massive intertextual reference. Try to forget the delightful film and let the language do its own work.

The chapter is framed by a title in italic typeface and set in speech marks indicating a voice uttering an imperative. Whose voice is it? There's another intertextual reference here to language used in fairgrounds and summer fetes. By the end of the chapter it is clear that 'my' refers to the pig.

Next, another voice asking a question. We don't know yet what the demonstrative 'that' refers to. Note the phrase beginning with the present participle, 'sticking' in this case, a familiar way of following up direct speech with narrative comment. Notice also the triple adjective string pre-modifying 'face', and that 'comfortable' has been placed first.

Mrs Hogget's speech style is conveyed very clearly by the comma splices. In A-Level essays, such a technique would be unsuitable, but here it works well. Notice dialectal and idiolectal features. There are quite a few exclamations too. It is nearly all exclamation and the questions are rhetorical.

In a new paragraph the narrator comments on the scene. Notice, once again, the effectiveness of a three word sentence. The paragraph is essentially a list following the colon. There are obvious parallelisms: three definite articles; three uses of 'very'. Notice the typical storyteller's use of pre-modification to build up to the word 'squealing' which leaves us in no doubt that it's all about a pig who has not appeared yet.

Notice how Farmer Hogget's taciturn speech style is contrasted with his wife's speech style. The phrase 'as big round' sounds like regional dialect yet it is in the narrative comment, not in the direct speech of a character.

Further remarks by Mrs Hogget in characteristic style. How well, speech style can convey character! Notice dialectal verb form 'knows' and eye-dialect (or phonetic spelling): 'thiseyer' Note also dialectal 'afore'.

'The squealing sounded again' – evidence of a storyteller knowing how to increase the suspense for the benefit of young and not-so-young readers already being drawn into an imagined world. Note repetition of 'That noise?'

Further comment from the narrator on his two characters, exemplified by Farmer Hogget's two single-word utterances ('Pig' and 'Yes') contrasted with a flow of comma spliced utterances from his wife who also nods a lot. Notice that Hogget is referred to as 'Farmer Hogget'.

There is a gap in the narrative, indicating a passage of time. Not dissimilar to the first excerpt from *Tess* there is a gradual focusing on a key character as the farmer walks toward the source of the squealing. Notice the climactic sentence, 'Inside was a little pig'.

Notice the old country word 'hefted' but notice especially the way in which the eye-to-eye contact is described. 'One saw . . .' is balanced (or parallelled) by 'and the other saw . . .' while the 'very long legs' are balanced (parallelled by 'very short ones'). This is verbal art. Colours are contrasted too. 'Long' and 'short' and 'thin' and 'fat' are antonyms – another example of foregrounding a feature.

Narratives contain implied as well as explicit meanings, and there is an implication here that Farmer Hogget and the pig have hit it off, right from the start.

More repetition, this time of 'carefully', an adverb which fronts three sentences in a row. Notice too that the SV grammatical pattern is parallelled. The two sentences beginning, 'Once again' are also parallelled, emphasising the dual focus now on the farmer and the pig.

Notice the delay in Farmer Hogget's decision – 'And a quarter'. Again character is economically conveyed through dialogue.

Notice the deliberate contrast of the pig's 'silence' when held by the farmer and the 'yelling' afterwards. Semantically, 'squealing' connotes animal sounds whereas 'yelling' connotes human sounds. Already the pig is becoming a personality, something a reader would expect from experience of a genre where anthropomorphism abounds.

The idea of 'never winning nothing' (double negatives which actually emphasise the statement) is repeated, which, coupled with the anaphoric reference to the telephone, tends to create anticipation and/or suspense.

If you were reading this aloud, failure to pause, to get the timing right, between the penultimate and the last paragraph, would be to miss completely an intended effect. This is a classic gap which the reader is perfectly able to fill in. The voice at the other end of the line (the vicar's) and the good news are left entirely unspoken.

If you want to understand something about the art as well as the linguistics of storytelling, read the story to a group of young children and watch how they react during the big pause. Then you will know exactly how to put the right expression into Farmer Hogget's 'Oh'.

You have looked at one very effective, highly controlled way of telling stories to children. The writing of the commentary above took much longer than it did to think through, but it should demonstrate to you how much goes on at very high speed, and all at once, in the mind of a reader drawn into a narrative. Your own thoughts and responses will be much quicker than you can write them.

**ACTIVITY 27**

Stylistics can point out a great many interesting features of a text, and, in this instance, can also give some guidelines for writing more imaginatively for children (and adults too!). A group of primary school teachers who love reading *The Sheep-Pig* to their classes were asked to say what qualities they enjoyed in the writing. Various responses were given: 'charm', 'warmth', 'wit', 'directness', 'sense of fun', 'it communicates'.

Consider one or two of these descriptions and identify stylistic features of the first chapter that create such impressions.

**ACTIVITY 28**

This activity is another exercise in style.

Write a chapter that could follow the first one from the *Sheep-Pig*. It should be mainly concerned with Mr Hogget collecting the pig and bringing it home to show Mrs Hogget. You may need to know that they also have a sheepdog. Keep the chapter brief, and make every effort to get out of your own idiolect and into the book's literary style.

Follow the author's example and be careful not to go overboard on accent and dialect. The things to go for are understatement, implication, nuances, economy.

# Short story writing

Short stories are as popular a form of prose fiction as novels. Apart from any qualities they may possess, they are very handy for putting in magazines, little pocket books and anthologies. A short story is more likely to be concerned with nuances of character, and possibly situation, than with intricacies of plot construction. It will be more likely to imply than to state, and it will tend to revelation rather than extended creation of effects.

## *Miss Brill by Katherine Mansfield*

**ACTIVITY 29**

In this activity you will have an opportunity to investigate a complete story, *Miss Brill*, by Katherine Mansfield (1888–1923). Read the story slowly, and listen to it inside your head. When you have read it once, read it again paying particular attention to the following:

- uses of certain words: sad, little, tiny, cupboard, chill
- ways in which thoughts are communicated
- use of theatrical references.

You should also note any other stylistic features.

ALTHOUGH it was so brilliantly fine – the blue sky powdered with gold and great spots of light like white wine splashed over the Jardins Publiques – Miss Brill was glad that she had decided on her fur. The air was motionless, but when you opened your mouth there was just a faint chill, like a chill from a glass of iced water before you sip, and now and again a leaf came drifting – from nowhere, from the sky. Miss Brill put up her hand and touched her fur. Dear little thing! It was nice to feel it again. She had taken it out of its box that afternoon, shaken out the moth-powder, given it a good brush, and rubbed the life back into the dim little eyes. 'What has been happening to me?' said the sad little eyes. Oh, how sweet it was to see them snap at her again from the red eiderdown! ... But the nose, which was of some black composition, wasn't at all firm. It must have had a knock, somehow. Never mind – a little dab of black sealing-wax when the time came – when it was absolutely necessary. ... Little rogue! Yes, she really felt like that about it. Little rogue biting its tail just by her left ear. She could have taken it off and laid it on her lap and stroked it. She felt a tingling in her hands and arms, but that came from walking, she supposed. And when she breathed, something light and sad – no, not sad, exactly – something gentle seemed to move in her bosom.

There were a number of people out this afternoon, far more than last Sunday. And the band sounded louder and gayer. That was because the Season had begun. For although the band played all the year round on Sundays, out of season it was never the same. It was like some one playing with only the family to listen; it didn't care how it played if there weren't any strangers present. Wasn't the conductor wearing a new coat, too? She was sure it was new. He scraped with his foot and flapped his arms like a rooster about to crow, and the bandsmen sitting in the green rotunda blew out their cheeks and glared at the music. Now there came a little 'flutey' bit – very pretty! – a little chain of bright drops. She was sure it would be repeated. It was; she lifted her head and smiled.

Only two people shared her 'special' seat: a fine old man in a velvet coat, his hands clasped over a huge carved walking-stick, and a big old woman, sitting upright, with a roll of knitting on her embroidered apron. They did not speak. This was disappointing, for Miss Brill always looked forward to the conversation. She had become really quite expert, she thought, at listening as though she didn't listen, at sitting in other people's lives just for a minute while they talked round here.

She glanced, sideways, at the old couple. Perhaps they would go soon. Last Sunday, too, hadn't been as interesting as usual. An Englishman and his wife, he wearing a dreadful Panama hat and she button boots. And she'd gone on the whole time about how she ought to wear spectacles; she knew she needed them; but that it was no good getting any; they'd be sure to break and they'd never keep on. And he'd been so patient. He'd suggested everything – gold rims, the kind that curved round your ears, little pads inside the bridge. No, nothing would please her. 'They'll always be sliding down my nose!' Miss Brill had wanted to shake her.

The old people sat on the bench, still as statues. Never mind, there was always the crowd to watch. To and fro, in front of the flower-beds and the band rotunda, the couples and groups paraded, stopped to talk, to greet, to buy a handful of flowers from the old beggar who had his tray fixed to the railings. Little children ran among them, swooping and laughing; little boys with big white silk bows under their chins, little girls, little French dolls, dressed up in velvet and lace. And sometimes a tiny staggerer came suddenly rocking into the open from under the trees, stopped, stared, as suddenly sat down 'flop', until its small high-stepping mother, like a young hen, rushed scolding to its rescue. Other people sat on the benches and green chairs, but they were nearly always the same, Sunday after Sunday, and – Miss Brill had often noticed – there was something funny about nearly all of them. They were odd, silent, nearly all old, and from the way they stared they looked as though they'd just come from dark little rooms or even – even cupboards!

Behind the rotunda the slender trees with yellow leaves down drooping, and through them just a line of sea, and beyond the blue sky with gold-veined clouds.

Tum-tum-tum tiddle-um! tiddle-um! tum tiddley-um tum ta! blew the band.

Two young girls in red came by and two young soldiers in blue met them, and they laughed and paired and went off arm-in-arm. Two pleasant women with funny straw hats passed, gravely, leading beautiful smoke-coloured donkeys. A cold, pale nun hurried by. A beautiful woman came along and dropped her bunch of violets, and a little boy ran after to hand them to her, and she took them and threw them away as if they'd been poisoned. Dear me! Miss Brill didn't know whether to admire that or not! And now an ermine toque and a gentleman in grey met just in front of her. He was tall, stiff, dignified, and she was wearing the ermine toque she'd bought when her hair was yellow. Now everything, her hair, her face, even her eyes, was the same colour as the shabby ermine, and her hand, in its cleaned glove, lifted to dab her lips, was a tiny yellowish paw. Oh, she was so pleased to see him – delighted! She rather thought they were going to meet that afternoon. She described where she'd been – everywhere, here, there, along by the sea. The day was so charming – didn't he agree? And wouldn't he, perhaps? ... But he shook his head, lighted a cigarette, slowly breathed a great deep puff into her face, and even while she was still talking and laughing, flicked the match away and walked on. The ermine toque was alone; she smiled more brightly than ever. But even the band seemed to know what she was feeling and played more softly, played tenderly, and the drum beat, 'The Brute! The Brute!' over and over. What would she do? What was going to happen now? But as Miss Brill wondered, the ermine toque turned, raised her hand as though she'd seen some one else, much nicer, just over there, and pattered away. And the band changed again and played more quickly, more gaily than ever, and the odd couple on Miss Brill's seat got up and marched away, and such a funny old man with long whiskers hobbled along in time to the music and was nearly knocked over by four girls walking abreast.

Oh, how fascinating it was! How she enjoyed it! How she loved sitting here, watching it all! It was like a play. It was exactly like a play. Who could believe the sky at the back wasn't painted? But it wasn't till a little brown dog trotted on solemn and then slowly trotted off, like a little 'theatre' dog, a little dog that had been drugged, that Miss Brill discovered what it was that made it so exciting. They were all on the stage. They weren't only the audience, not only looking on; they were acting. Even she had a part and came every Sunday. No doubt somebody would have noticed if she hadn't been there; she was part of the performance after all. How strange she'd never thought of it like that before! And yet it explained why she made such a point of starting from home at just the same time each week – so as not to be late for the performance – and it also explained why she had quite a queer, shy feeling at telling her English pupils how she spent her Sunday afternoons. No wonder! Miss Brill nearly laughed out loud. She was on the stage. She thought of the old invalid gentleman to whom she read the newspaper four afternoons a week while he slept in the garden. She had got quite used to the frail head on the cotton pillow, the hollowed eyes, the open mouth and the high pinched nose. If he'd been dead she mightn't have noticed for weeks; she wouldn't have minded. But suddenly he knew he was having the paper read to him by an actress! 'An actress!' The old head lifted; two points of light quivered in the old eyes. 'An actress – are ye?' And Miss Brill smoothed the newspaper as though it were the manuscript of her part and said gently: 'Yes, I have been an actress for a long time.'

The band had been having a rest. Now they started again. And what they played was warm, sunny, yet there was just a faint chill – a something what was it? – not sadness – no, not sadness – a something that made you want to sing. The tune lifted, lifted, the light shone; and it seemed to Miss Brill that in another moment all of them, all the whole company, would begin singing. The young ones, the laughing ones who were moving together, they would begin, and the men's voices, very resolute and brave, would join them. And then she too, she too, and the others on the benches – they would come in with a kind of accompaniment – something low, that scarcely rose or fell, something so beautiful – moving. . . . And Miss Brill's eyes filled with tears and she looked smiling at all the other members of the company. Yes, we understand, we understand, she thought – though what they understood she didn't know.

Just at that moment a boy and a girl came and sat down where the old couple had been. They were beautifully dressed; they were in love. The hero and heroine, of course, just arrived from his father's yacht. And still soundlessly singing, still with that trembling smile, Miss Brill prepared to listen.

'No, not now,' said the girl. 'Not here, I can't.'

'But why? Because of that stupid old thing at the end there?' asked the boy. 'Why does she come here at all – who wants her? Why doesn't she keep her silly old mug at home?'

'Its her fu-fur which is so funny,' giggled the girl. 'It's exactly like a fried whiting.'

'Ah, be off with you!' said the boy in an angry whisper. Then: 'Tell me, ma petite chère –'

'No, not here,' said the girl. 'Not *yet*.'

On her way home she usually bought a slice of honey-cake at the baker's. It was her Sunday treat. Sometimes there was an almond in her slice, sometimes not. It made a great difference. If there was an almond it was like carrying home a tiny present – a surprise – something that might very well not have been there. She hurried on the almond Sundays and struck the match for the kettle in quite a dashing way.

But to-day she passed the baker's by, climbed the stairs, went into the little dark room – her room like a cupboard – and sat down on the red eiderdown. She sat there for a long time. The box that the fur came out of was on the bed. She unclasped the necklet quickly; quickly, without looking, laid it inside. But when she put the lid on she thought she heard something crying.

## COMMENTARY

The text of *Miss Brill* is very finely crafted and the following remarks take the form of a running commentary reflecting one reader's journey throughout the text. Sometimes a running commentary is a good technique for getting into the details of a text. It is a way of thinking, writing and earning marks at the same time.

The important thing is that you are really making comments and observations and not merely paraphrasing. The word 'notice' is often useful; indeed beginning to notice more and more is a sign of making progress in stylistics. Here it is being used to draw your attention to features of the language but you can legitimately use it to direct and examine and notice something you think is significant. One stylistic effect it will have on your writing is that it introduces an imperative sentence or two into your answer conveying that you are in control of what is going on. Answers that consist entirely of running commentary can earn many marks if the comments are interesting but they are not entirely satisfactory. Ideally you want to achieve a blend of really good comment with more extended discussion and evaluation of the points you think most important. So, here is a running commentary on *Miss Brill.*

The story begins with an 'Although . . .'. Without wishing to put too fine a point on it, the word does introduce a touch of exactness. The dependent and main clauses are separated by a long parenthesis – further precision of detail. Parentheses and afterthoughts punctuated by dashes are a fairly frequent feature of this text.

Close association of Miss Brill with the fur occurs right at the start and at the very end of the story. The eyes of the fur are given a direct voice: 'What has been happening to me?' or so Miss Brill imagines. Note use of 'little': little eyes (twice), little rogue (twice).

Note the second person pronoun in 'when you opened your mouth'. Does this have the effect of including the reader in the experience?

The word 'sad' is used three times in the opening paragraph. Note too the qualification 'no, not sad, exactly'. Miss Brill's thoughts in the first paragraph are expressed as free indirect thoughts.

Note inverted commas for 'flutey' and 'special'. More evidence of discrimination on the part of the writer, making it clear that these are Miss Brill's own words, not the narrator's. Notice long sentence followed by short one: 'They did not speak'. More free indirect thought: 'Perhaps they would go soon' and, 'Never mind'. Note free direct speech: 'They'll always be sliding down my nose' followed by free indirect thought from Miss Brill.

Note:

- more 'littles' in paragraph five
- 'Staggerer' looks like author's own word
- the word 'cupboards' at the end.

Paragraph five is followed by, first a pictorial paragraph, then a short sound paragraph. Notice the parallelisms in paragraph eight: 'Two young girls in red . . .'.

Note the effect created by 'the ermine toque turned . . .'. What effect does this kind of metonymy have on the way a reader views the woman wearing the ermine toque? Is it the way Miss Brill views her? Notice Miss Brill's thoughts, 'The Brute' and 'such a funny old man'. What is the effect of the adverb 'such'? What does it communicate?

Paragraph ten develops the idea of acting in a play, mostly in the form of free indirect thought. Free direct thought would be in the present tense, this is all in the past tense and concludes with direct speech: 'Yes, I have been an actress for a long time'.

Paragraph 11 repeats two thematic words used earlier: 'chill' and 'sad'. Note also the repetition of 'she too'. What effect does this have? At the end, Miss Brill's thoughts are reported by the narrator, 'we understand'. But whose thought is: 'what they understood she didn't know'. Miss Brill's or the narrator's? Note also the elision, 'didn't', and the use, on the only occasion, of the first person plural.

The adverb 'just' in an initial position of both sentence and new paragraph, introduces a suddenness, an immediacy, into the timescale of the story.

Note the parallelism of: 'They were beautifully dressed; they were in love'. The conversation, the only conventionally presented direct speech in the story, is introduced: '. . . Miss Brill prepared to listen.' In view of the content of the ensuing conversation you may feel even more intensely, the poignancy of the narrator's description and the agony that follows. After the girl's final remark, there is a notable narrative gap. There is no need for the storyteller to fill it in to elaborate on the shock; readers can be trusted to feel the shock for themselves.

Notice how the 'almond' is the principal theme word of the penultimate paragraph, and how, by drawing the reader's attention to that, as to the fur, the narrator can say much about Miss Brill by implication. Writers need not go for a full, frontal description of characters' feelings; more can often be achieved by this kind of displacement. It is an example of implied meaning.

The story has a very strong sense of an ending; the narrative is 'closed' every bit as finally as the replacing of the lid on the fur's box. The last sentence is, however, ambiguous. Some readers see it as a fanciful thought, in keeping with other thoughts of Miss Brill's; others interpret it as telling the reader that Miss Brill is crying. The great thing about a good story is that you can have it both ways without contradiction. A favourite cohesive strategy (connecting and progressing bits of narrative) is the use of 'And' in the initial sentence position (nine times). The word 'but' is also used in the initial position several times and to begin the final sentence of all.

Notice how the frequency and placing of the word 'little' leads the reader to a perception of what might be called 'the little world of Miss Brill'. Even the almond at the end is a 'tiny present'. You might also consider that the word conveys by implication, something of preference and power. Little things in life, Miss Brill can control and manage. The adjective 'little' has the effect of diminishing whatever comes next. It often irritates when overused. Psychologically, it can plead, persuade, lessen, reassure, mislead or imply submission.

The use of the word 'sad' is almost an explicit comment on Miss Brill's life, so insistently is it used. Twice, there is a discrimination: 'no, not sad, exactly' and 'no, not sadness'. The first is qualified by the word 'gentle', the second by, 'something that made you want to sing' – both deeply ironic given her experience on that day in the park.

The word 'cupboard' has a chilling effect. Notice how it is quite closely collocated with 'dark little room' early in the story and then again in the final paragraph.

The word 'chill' occurs very early in the story, 'a faint chill' and it seems inevitable that the words 'now and again a leaf came drifting' will connote Autumn in most readers' minds. There is also a 'faint chill' in the music. The word is bound to echo in a reader's response to the story – as in the comment above about 'cupboard'. It contrasts with antonyms used about the music, 'warm, sunny' and provides a reason for the fur which has a symbolic as well as actual relevance to the story. Is it merely coincidence that 'chill' is the one word in the story that rhymes with 'Brill'?

In the commentary so far, references have been made to Miss Brill's thoughts because, clearly, they are an essential, if not *the* essential, part of the story.

Storytellers have at their disposal both explicit and implicit means of conveying information and attitudes to readers. It is helpful, for example, to be told about the competition to guess the pig's weight, just as it is helpful to know about Miss Brill's fur. Readers do not need to be told however, the substance of the telephone message, or how hurt and devastated Miss Brill felt at the young man's cruel words. They know these things by implication.

The handling of thoughts is a subtle business in fiction. Katherine Mansfield conveys not only Miss Brill's thoughts, giving her an identity of her own in the narrative, she also conveys the narrator's thoughts. Sometimes the reader is inside Miss Brill's mind – seeing things through her ways of thinking and with her attitudes: 'Miss Brill had wanted to shake her' and 'The Brute!' At other times the reader sees things through the narrator's eyes and mind: 'still with that trembling smile' and 'her room like a cupboard'.

Slipping in and out of Miss Brill's thoughts while maintaining a distinct narrative voice is part of the author's achievement. You will appreciate this linguistic achievement all the more if you try one or two exercises or experiments in style.

---

We do have a commentary by the author herself on *Miss Brill*. In a letter to a friend, in 1921, she wrote the following:

'It's a very queer thing how craft comes into writing. I mean down to details ... In *Miss Brill* I chose not only the length of every sentence, but even the sound of every sentence. I chose the rise and fall of every paragraph to fit her, and to fit on that day at that very moment. After I'd written it I read it aloud – numbers of times – just as one would play over a musical composition – trying to get it nearer and nearer to the expression of Miss Brill – until it fitted her.

'Don't think I am vain about this little sketch. It's only the method I wanted to explain. I often wonder whether other writers do the same – if a thing has really come off it seems to me there mustn't be one single word out of place, or one word that could be taken out. That's how I aim my writing. It will take some time to get anywhere near there.'

**ACTIVITY 30**

Re-write the opening section (about 14 lines) in the first person from Miss Brill's point of view. Write in the past tense: 'Although it was so brilliantly fine . . . I was glad I had decided on my fur'.

When you have done this, consider what difficulties (for example, possible clumsiness) this approach might cause when relating the scene with the young lovers.

Now try the 'stream of consciousness' approach, using the first person and the present tense. This is a form of free, direct thought: 'Even though it is so brilliantly fine . . . there's a faint chill in the air . . . I'm glad I decided to put my fur on... Dear little thing! It is so nice to feel it again'.

Now re-write a section removing the free, indirect speech altogether and maintaining a narrative distance from the character. You could remove, for example her thoughts about the fur in the first paragraph, or her thoughts about the music. Read the altered version, beginning with the preceding passage and including the following paragraph. What difference does it make?

Now write in your own words the advantages to be gained from the use of free indirect speech in fictional narrative.

Language, whether in everyday forms or in literary imagination, never seems to stay very long in the literal vein. Figurative language, especially metaphor, seems to lie in wait in the imagination. At the literal level, the narrative of *Miss Brill* tells the reader that she sits in her room, she goes to sit in the park and she returns to sit in her room. Other people come and go, and the band plays on. Yet alongside all the explicit, concrete, common nouns adjectives and verbs the author uses to depict and narrate, there are other words from an alternative, metaphorical semantic field, namely acting and the theatre. First, the simile: 'It was like a play', repeated. Then, in quick succession: 'painted scenery', 'theatre dog', 'on the stage', 'audience', 'she had a part', 'performance', 'an actress', 'accompaniment', 'the hero and heroine', 'members of the company'.

These all introduce a new dimension of meaning and as Miss Brill sees everybody taking part in a play, so does the reader, except that readers also see the play in which Miss Brill has not yet realised she too is playing a part. Her own life, by implication, is playacting on a 'little' stage.

It is important in literary stylistics to observe both literal and metaphorical uses of language, especially when metaphorical uses influence so powerfully the reader's interpretation of the literal.

The effect created here can be described as 'the watcher watched' – a well known literary and cinematic device. In *Miss Brill* it works in two ways. On the one hand, Miss Brill is the observer, the spectator in the park, 'sitting in other people's lives', when suddenly she becomes the object of somebody else's unflattering gaze. On the other hand, Miss Brill has always been under close observation by the narrator herself, and in turn by the spectator reader.

**ACTIVITY 31**

Describe in about fifty words the feelings and attitudes of Katherine Mansfield you detect in her narrative voice.

**ACTIVITY 32**

Write a brief, biographical portrait of Miss Brill based solely on information stated or implied in the text. Alternatively, write a description of Miss Brill as seen from the point of view of someone else sitting in the park that day. It could be sympathetic or mildly comic.

**ACTIVITY 33**

Keeping as closely as possible to the style of Katherine Mansfield, write about a later visit to the park by Miss Brill. There's a hint of Autumn in Mansfield's story, what season will you choose? Will she wear the fur again?

# A sense of an ending

**ACTIVITY 34**

There follow two excerpts from prose fiction. Read them and carry out the following:

1 Write a brief account of first impressions of genre, content, style, organisation and anything else that interests you.
2 Write a detailed running commentary on features of the text.
3 Identify and discuss an aspect of prose fiction you find particularly relevant to each excerpt.
4 Compare the two texts for similarities and differences.

In the first text Julia has returned to the apartment in Vienna where she had hidden and nursed her ailing Jewish husband, Franz, throughout the Nazi occupation. Her maid Fina and her husband have met their deaths at the hands of Russian soldiers.

In the second, Margaret has moved to the north of England and become aware of great social as well as geographical differences in Victorian England. The book is also a love story in which Margaret is finally united with the man she loves, Mr Thornton, whose grim and intolerant family owns a cotton mill.

This time you are looking at the final pages of the novels:

The first is *Night Falls On The City* by Sarah Gainham (1967)

The second is from *North and South* by Mrs Gaskell (1854–55)

You could extend this activity by acquiring a copy of Hardy's *Tess of the D'Urbervilles* and looking at the concluding pages. Tess has been hanged for the murder of Alec D'Urberville. Begin at: 'up this road from the precincts of the city two persons were walking...'.

**(i)**

Presently she got up and went into the living-room, driven by the need to know, to probe – to know what, she did not ask herself. The books struck her first; many were missing and in the gaps the dark woodwork showed gloomily in the long rows. Those on the shelves were in unfamiliar places, many upside down. About the useless stove were piled others, some that belonged here and some that did not; from their titles she supposed they had been collected from all over the house, including the attorney's office for some of them were law books. At the windows, intact here for the shell had glanced off the outer wall between the salon and her own room, were clean curtains of her own coarse linen net although the velvet overcurtains were missing. All had been carefully cleaned, a long rent in the carpet mended with long, cobbling stiches; the rugs bought one after another to cover shabby patches were now laid in unfamiliar places at odd angles and one of them was not hers. This no longer puzzled her as the bedside lamp had done; she knew now that things had been gathered together, the place put in order as well as it could be by people who had never before seen it. The door in the panelling to the dining-room hung loose with a hinge missing, the lock forced. She did not remember locking the dining-room but it was so long since it had been used that it could well have been locked for months; the months spent waking and sleeping here before going to the cellar. The clumsy iron cooker, its enamel covering chipped and starred, still stood in the corner and its pipe, already rusting, disappeared botched into the discoloured wall. At the stove end the wall was papered, there were no book-shelves there, and the whole buckets of heaven knew what had been flung against it. The room still smelled of antiseptics from its hasty cleaning. There were no flowers, of course, and the Meissen vase had lost one snake handle; there was a long crack winding across its upper curve. The pictures from between the windows were gone.

On the big flat desk there was nothing left. Its scratched, much-used surface gleamed dully, quite blank. Not even the ink-wells and pen rack of green marble, never used, were there. All the locks were broken. The drawers were empty. Every single piece of paper, every notebook was gone. Even unused paper was gone, even the pencils and fountain pens, the copy pencils, the stapler with a lion on its grip, the folders, the file of letters. Here there had been no attempt to put anything back in place; the desk had been totally cleared. The chair was intact and she sat down in it and rested her elbows on the arm rests, her clasped hands lying before her on the surface of the empty desk. I wonder what happened to my rings, she thought indifferently.

All this no longer belonged to her, just as the glittering rings were no longer hers. This empty desk was not what was left of lives or objects that once had content and meaning. It had no relation to anything and might have been a piece of furniture in a hired furnished room.

She tried to push her thoughts back to her rings. Where had she last had them, remembered having them? The unconscious tricks she had been playing no longer worked. She looked at the unbelievable fact now, and could not avoid it. Not only the desk was empty, it had all gone for nothing. The shifts, the struggle, the sacrifice of Fina who had been nothing else but victim, even though the victim of her own female self-sacrifice; the deceit, the responsibility, were all nothing. There was nothing left of Franz; she was alone in a new life and world, as she was alone in this apartment. A world so strange that it had as yet not even a form; and certainly, all content being gone into nothingness, no content.

As the doctor said, nothing was her own any more and nothing would be as it had been before. There was only one question left in the void of meaning: how could it happen that she had been forced to survive?

Meaning, reality, retreated from its containing form backward into the primitive dark of a cave underground and in an instant of mindless uproar, was gone. And those who finalised the breakdown into chaos, its unknowing and unmeaning agents who now inherited the empty space, attempted by filling shelves with books turned upside down to refill the monstrous emptiness. Chaos claimed meaning and destroyed it; immediately the unknowable content was to be replaced by object put into what might seem like their proper order. The bloody tattered flesh was sewn together, cosseted and serviced back into a semblance of meaning so that it could be exposed in public as incontrovertible evidence of the survival of what had been destroyed.

She became aware that if there was no meaning there was still sensation. As healed wounds do, the long scar on her head began to itch and, remembering the nuns' warnings not to scratch, she rubbed it gently with her fingertips. She had not yet seen this scar and wondered vaguely whether she would carry a visible mark; but she was too exhausted to get up and trail back into the bedroom where there was a looking-glass that would show her what she looked like.

**(ii)**

Mr Thornton did not speak, and she went on looking for some paper on which were written down the proposals for security; for she was most anxious to have it all looked upon in the light of a mere business arrangement, in which the principal advantage would be on her side. While she sought for this paper, her very heart-pulse was arrested by the tone in which Mr Thornton spoke. His voice was hoarse, and trembling with tender passion, as he said:

'Margaret!'

For an instant she looked up; and then sought to veil her luminous eyes by dropping her forehead on her hands. Again, stepping nearer, he besought her with another tremulous eager call upon her name.

'Margaret!'

Still lower went the head: more closely hidden was the face, almost resting on the table before her. He came close to her. He knelt by her side, to bring his face to a level with her ear; and whispered – panted out the words:

'Take care. – If you do not speak – I shall claim you as my own in some strange presumptuous way. – Send me away at once, if I must go; – Margaret! –'

At that third call she turned her face, still covered with her small white hands, towards him, and laid it on his shoulder, hiding it even there; and it was too delicious to feel her soft cheek against his, for him to wish to see either deep blushes or loving eyes. He clasped her close. But they both kept silence. At length she murmured in a broken voice:

'Oh, Mr Thornton, I am not good enough!'

'Not good enough! Don't mock my own deep feeling of unworthiness.'

After a minute or two, he gently disengaged her hands from her face, and laid her arms as they had once before been placed to protect him from the rioters.

'Do you remember, love?' he murmured. 'And how I requited you with my insolence the next day?'

'I remember how wrongly I spoke to you, – that is all.'

'Look here! Lift up your head. I have something to show you!' She slowly faced him, glowing with beautiful shame.

'Do you know these roses?' he said, drawing out his pocket-book, in which were treasured up some dead flowers.

'No!' she replied, with innocent curiosity. 'Did I give them to you?'

'No! Vanity; you did not. You may have worn sister roses very probably.'

She looked at them, wondering for a minute, then she smiled a little as she said –

'They are from Helstone, are they not? I know the deep indentations round the leaves. Oh! have you been there? When were you there?'

'I wanted to see the place where Margaret grew to what she is, even at the worst time of all, when I had no hope of ever calling her mine. I went there on my return from Havre.'

'You must give them to me,' she said, trying to take them out of his hand with gentle violence.

'Very well. Only you must pay me for them!'

'How shall I ever tell aunt Shaw?' she whispered, after some time of delicious silence.

'Let me speak to her.'

'Oh, no! I owe to her, – but what will she say?'

'I can guess. Her first exclamation will be, "That man!"'

'Hush!' said Margaret, 'or I shall try and show you your mother's indignant tones as she says, "That woman!" '

# Summary

In this chapter you have considered many of the factors that construct or weave together a fictional story:

- narrative point of view
- the role of conversation
- implied meanings
- narrative pace and pause
- varieties of speech and thought within a narrative.

# 4 The Poetic Muse

## Survey

This chapter looks at poetry, and considers the following topics:

- clichés and poetic expression
- *The Cool Web*, a poem about language
- *Love is more thicker*, an analysis of 'deviant' language
- A Shakespeare sonnet
- modern 'light' verse
- traditional 'heavy' verse
- poetry and graphology
- *The Sick Rose* and symbolism
- *Spelling*, another poet reflecting on language.

In working through a series of activities connected to these topics, you will develop your skills in stylistics by looking at extremely concise, ambiguous, highly inferential and finely crafted forms of language.

## Poetry and Muses

The following are lines from sonnets by Sir Philip Sidney (1554–86):

" 'Fool!' said my Muse, to me, 'look in thy heart, and write'."

"Muses scorn with vulgar brains to dwell."

The idea of poetry as something inspired by muses (or Muses) is an ancient one. The word 'muse' came into the language from Greek and Latin, via French. It refers to the mythical source of both music and poetry, and given the importance of phonological features of poetry, this association with sounds should not be surprising. The traditional muses are three, all female:

- Aoide, the muse of song;
- Melete, the muse of meditation; and
- Mneme, the muse of memory (hence the word 'mnemonics').

Later writers have added to the number of muses; there is even one for comedy, Thalia. The idea of a tenth muse is relatively modern and refers to industry, science and technology.

Looking at *Ozymandias*, *Westminster Bridge* and *The Holy Sonnet* it is not difficult to see the appropriateness of the three traditional muses as inspirations in all three poems: outburst of song; reflection and meditation ('musing', if you like); and recollections of past events in life and history.

Ancient theories of poetic inspiration by spirits sounds very much at odds with modern stylistics. One weakness in them is that they place too much emphasis on the poet as inspired meaning-maker and not enough on the reader. This might be another way of saying that if there are such things as muses they inspire readers' imaginations too. When people read poetry, they expect something thoughtful, something that 'sounds' good, and something memorable. It is important therefore to recognise these aspects of poetry and not to kill them stone dead by a resolutely analytical approach to texts.

In 1960, Roman Jakobson, pointed out the combined folly of 'a linguist deaf to the poetic function and a literary scholar indifferent to linguistic problems and unconversant with linguistic methods'. In 1972 David Crystal stated, 'The stylistician must thoroughly appreciate the literary critic's position.'

## *Clichés*

There is a mainstream view, stemming from linguists like Jakobson, that in its poetic function, language deviates from norms and conventions of everyday use. It is language that draws attention to itself and is concerned more overtly with matters of form. Obvious examples you have met so far are the conscious use of repetition, parallelisms, and foregrounding. You have also observed imaginative effects in fictional narratives (the poetic function isn't confined to verse). If literature in general is thought of as a deviating use of language, then poetry seems the most deviant of all, using carefully crafted metre, tightly organised methods of formal construction, complex ways of making meanings and, at first sight, obscure ways of communicating them. Poetry breaks all of Grice's maxims.

An important reason for this 'deviance' is the fact that the common corpus of language that we share and use everyday, is both an advantage for communication yet a serious constraint on originality of expression. The word 'cliché' is frequently used to describe well-worn, over familiar expressions. The following are all clichés:

- 'take life as it comes'
- 'look for the silver lining'
- 'death comes to us all'
- 'love is just around the corner'.

There is nothing dreadfully wrong with clichés; they are fine at the right time in the right place. But they are examples of the kind of language that comes to mind automatically. Poets, novelists and playwrights, usually seek original expressions rather than clichés or hackneyed sayings, for the satisfaction of saying something in a way that seems (to them) exactly right. The two quotations at the beginning of this chapter illustrate something of this. Really saying what is in your heart is not easy but it is where the originality or the interest lies. The opening reference to 'vulgar minds' shouldn't be interpreted as Elizabethan snobbery, but rather as a reference to the common corpus mentioned earlier. Poets try to say things differently and in a voice that they feel is true to themselves.

**ACTIVITY 35**

Write down ten or so well known clichés and ask:

**1** Why is each one useful?

**2** Where some of them might have originated?

Choose one and express the thought behind it in words of your own.

**ACTIVITY 36**

Just as clichés and stereotypes can be useful in everyday talk, they can also be enjoyable as light entertainment. In both cases it is the degree of moderation in use and awareness that they are clichés and stereotypes that make all the difference. Look again at the three Fleming excerpts. Unlike the excerpts from Dickens, Hardy, Shelley, Wordsworth and Donne, there is no distinctive, authorial voice in any of these excerpts. They are clever, entertaining, very professional representations of a particular genre. Certainly many readers make a distinction of this kind between 'serious' imaginative literature (verbal art) and verbal art primarily written to entertain in a particular genre. The novelist Graham Greene refers to some of his stories as 'entertainments'. What clichés and stereotypes of the genre do you recognise in the three Fleming excerpts? Do you detect a 'voice' at all?

## *The Cool Web by Robert Graves*

**ACTIVITY 37**

Look now at the poem, *The Cool Web* by Robert Graves. Examine first the kinds of imagery he introduces into the poem, noting in particular any oppositions or antonyms. What kind of a 'world' is created inside your own head? Then write a statement of what you think the poet is saying about language and life – assuming you agree that that is what the poem is about. Remember that Ian Fleming is activating a formula that he knows he can make work very well, whereas Graves is trying to put into words something not quite so easy to find words for, hence a degree of 'obscurity'.

## The Cool Web

Children are dumb to say how hot the day is,
How hot the scent is of the summer rose,
How dreadful the black wastes of evening sky,
How dreadful the tall soldiers drumming by.

But we have speech, to chill the angry day,
And speech, to dull the rose's cruel scent.
We spell away the overhanging night,
We spell away the soldiers and the fright.

There's a cool web of language winds us in,
Retreat from too much joy or too much fear:
We grow sea-green at last and coldly die
In brininess and volubility.

But if we let our tongues lose self-possession,
Throwing off language and its watery clasp
Before our death, instead of when death comes,
Facing the wide glare of the children's day,
Facing the rose, the dark sky and the drums,
We shall go mad no doubt and die that way.

**COMMENTARY**

The title is a slightly surprising adjective/noun collocation that requires explanation. Is the reader going to get one? A quick scan of the poem's surface structure reveals five sentences set out in four verses (4 lines +4 +4 +6). The lines are decasyllabic with a noticeable but irregular rhyming scheme.

The first verse makes a statement, 'Children are dumb' and there is repetition in 'how hot' and 'How dreadful'.

The second verse begins with a 'But . . .' signalling contradiction or modification. 'Speech' and 'spell away' are repeated. The introduction of the idea of 'spells' (magic incantation) is intriguing.

Three themes in the first verse are also repeated: the rose, the night sky and the soldiers – not unfamiliar poetic themes or images.

'Hot' in the first verse is contrasted with 'chill' in the second and both are inevitably understood by the reader in the context of 'cool' in the title, for that is the linguistic effect of titles – they pre-modify everything.

The third verse specifically introduces and explains the 'cool web' of the title. It presents the idea of language as an element in which we exist, a cold, unexciting retreat from 'too much' intensity in life.

The last verse also begins with a 'But . . .' (another pattern). The first verse themes (rose, dark sky, soldiers) are repeated and the poet explicitly states that without language we would go mad.

A look back over the poem reveals six uses of the pronoun 'we', two uses of 'our' and one use of 'us'. There is a strong third person plural presence here, identifying poet and readers.

It is interesting that a poet should muse upon the relationship between language (his stock in trade) and reality ('too much joy or too much fear'). Another poet, T. S. Eliot has remarked that 'man cannot bear too much reality'. Notice that the primaeval idea of immersion in water is also a part of the poem as well as the idea of being caught in a web.

The poem also offers an unusual point of view on language acquisition as a process of learning to put into words, or 'spell out', the things that overwhelm or frighten us, in order to gain control over them and subdue them in our imaginations.

## ACTIVITY 38

Graves' poem is about the power of language to subdue fears and it also demonstrates one way in which a poet will attempt to use language to put difficult feelings and ideas into words. The next poem, less conventional in a variety of ways, also demonstrates a poet's attempt to put something difficult into words. Whereas Graves observes standard forms of punctuation, lexical choice and grammar, e. e. cummings does not.

Read the poem (remember to listen to it as well) and make notes on the following:

1 The ways in which rules are broken.
2 Features in the poem that show extreme control and organisation
3 The use of conventional images (clichés?) found in love poems.

## *love is more thicker than forget by E. E. Cummings*

love is more thicker than forget
more thinner than recall
more seldom than a wave is wet
more frequent than to fail

it is most mad and moonly
and less it shall unbe
than all the sea which only
is deeper than the sea

love is less always than to win
less never than alive
less bigger than the least begin
less littler than forgive

it is most sane and sunly
and more it cannot die
than all the sky which only
is higher than the sky

## *Shall I compare thee to a summer's day by William Shakespeare*

**ACTIVITY 39**

Now read the following love sonnet by William Shakespeare which belongs to, and has in turn influenced, a long tradition of love poetry.

Shall I compare thee to a summer's day?
Thou art more lovely and more temperate:
Rough winds do shake the darling buds of May,
And summer's lease hath all too short a date:
Sometimes too hot the eye of heaven shines,
And often is his gold complexion dimmed;
And every fair from fair sometimes declines,
By chance or nature's changing course untrimmed;
But thy eternal summer shall not fade,
Nor lose possession of that fair thou ow'st;
Nor shall death brag thou wander'st in his shade,
When in eternal lines to time thou grow'st:
So long as men can breathe, or eyes can see,
So long lives this, and this gives life to thee.

How does the poem by E. E. Cummings relate to the Shakespeare sonnet? Start by considering the word 'compare'.

**COMMENTARY**

A preliminary scan of the Cummings poem reveals four unpunctuated verses corresponding to four sentences.

The poem consists of a series of statements that are syntactically simple in verses one and three, and complex in two and four. In either case the directness is easy to read without conventional punctuation. Verse one consists of four statements in parallel with a single subject/verb combination, for example, 'Love is'.

This pattern is repeated in verse three. Once two verses are compared in this way, an extraordinary tight cohesion becomes evident. Note the antonyms contrasted in these two verses: 'more' with 'less'. Note too the antonyms within each verse: 'thicker/thinner'; 'seldom/frequent'; 'forget/recall'; and 'always/never'; 'bigger/littler'. The more you look through the other verses, the more antonymy you will find.

The grammatical difference between verses two and four is the use of a relative clause beginning with 'which'. A grammatical feature running through all four verses is the use of 'than'. The function of both of these features is to enable comparison, as indeed is the function of all the contrasted adverbs (more/less/most) and the comparative form adjectives (thicker/higher).

In effect, the poem shows how impossible it is for words to express a deep love. We make comparisons as best we can with the language available. Shakespeare's sonnet, written at the height of a tradition of extravagant love poetry seems to acknowledge the very impossibility of adequate comparison when it asks, 'Shall I compare thee to a summer's day?' Cummings' poem looks back on that tradition of passionate comparison and comes to the same conclusion. Language is, on the one hand, stretched to breaking point, yet on the other, is brilliantly crafted into a little gem, needing no title, no punctuation and no explanation.

Frequently, the satisfaction to be derived from literary stylistics, or investigating verbal art, is the recognition of how much triumph there is in making the words do something just a little bit fresh, authentic, original, instead of letting unconsidered clichés take over.

## *Witty Poems*

Some poems originate in a spirit of linguistic playfulness, others in more reflective moods. Poems may also be a mixture of the comic and the serious. The activities that follow give you an opportunity to examine ways in which language is used to achieve humorous as well as poetic effects.

### ACTIVITY 40

**To Someone Who Insisted I Look Up Someone**

I rang them up while touring Timbuctoo,
Those bosom chums to whom you're known as
'*Who?*'

X. J. KENNEDY (b. 1929)

**London Airport**

Last night in London Airport
I saw a wooden bin
labelled UNWANTED LITERATURE
IS TO BE PLACED HEREIN.
So I wrote a poem
and popped it in.

CHRISTOPHER LOGUE (b. 1926)

A very good way of understanding more fully the cleverness of these poems is to write something similar yourself. First work out what the 'recipe' would be for writing each poem. So, for your version of *To Someone Who Insisted I Look Up Someone*, make a long title; take two decasyllabic lines that rhyme; think of a home-truth about a commonplace situation; be a little bit witty. For each poem, follow as strictly as possible, the 'recipe'.

## *Two poems by Milton*

### ACTIVITY 41

The poet John Milton (1608–74) wrote two contrasting poems to which he gave Italian titles: *L'Allegro* and *Il Penseroso*. One is about being cheerful and good humoured, the other about being serious and sad. They reflect moods that alternate in most people's lives and also describe two broad categories of poetry.

Read the opening sections of each of the following poems. You will certainly notice a great deal of language change that has occurred in English poetry between then and now. You may even find the language archaic, and not particularly comprehensible. The enjoyment factor of reading the poems may initially be very low. Your main purpose however is to get at the voice behind the words and to identify the varieties of language strategies used by the poet.

# L'Allegro

Hence loathéd Melancholy
Of Cerberus and blackest midnight born,
In Stygian cave forlorn
'Mongst horrid shapes, and shrieks, and sights unholy,
Find out some uncouth cell,
Where brooding Darkness spreads his jealous wings,
And the night-raven sings;
There under ebon shades, and low-browed rocks,
As ragged as thy locks,
In dark Cimmerian desert ever dwell.
But come thou goddess fair and free,
In Heaven yclept Euphrosyne,
And by men, heart-easing Mirth,
Whom lovely Venus at a birth
With two sister Graces more
To ivy-crownéd Bacchus bore;
Or whether (as some sager sing)
The frolic wind that breathes the spring,
Zephyr with Aurora playing,
As he met her once a-Maying,
There on beds of violets blue,
And fresh-blown roses washed in dew,
Filled her with thee a daughter fair,
So buxom, blithe, and debonair.
Haste thee nymph, and bring with thee
Jest and youthful Jollity,
Quips and Cranks, and wanton Wiles,
Nods, and Becks, and wreathéd Smiles,
Such as hang on Hebe's cheek,
And love to live in dimple sleek;
Sport that wrinkled Care derides,
And Laughter, holding both his sides.
Come, and trip it as ye go
On the light fantastic toe,
And in thy right hand lead with thee,
The mountain nymph, sweet Liberty;
And if I give thee honor due,
Mirth, admit me of thy crew
To live with her and live with thee,
In unreprovéd pleasures free;
To hear the lark begin his flight,
And, singing, startle the dull night,
From his watch-tower in the skies,
Till the dappled dawn doth rise;
Then to come in spite of sorrow,
And at my window bid good morrow,
Through the sweetbriar, or the vine,
Or the twisted eglantine.

# Il Penseroso

Hence vain deluding Joys,
The brood of Folly without father bred.
How little you bestead,
Or fill the fixéd mind with all your toys;
Dwell in some idle brain,
And fancies fond with gaudy shapes possess,
As thick and numberless
As the gay motes that people the sunbeams,
Or likest hovering dreams,
The fickle pensioners of Morpheus' train.
But hail thou Goddess, sage and holy,
Hail, divinest Melancholy,
Whose saintly visage is too bright
To hit the sense of human sight;
And therefore to our weaker view,
O'erlaid with black, staid Wisdom's hue.
Black, but such as in esteem,
Prince Memnon's sister might beseem,
Or that starred Ethiope queen that strove
To set her beauty's praise above
The sea nymphs, and their powers offended.
Yet thou art higher far descended;
Thee bright-haired Vesta long of yore
To solitary Saturn bore;
His daughter she (in Saturn's reign)
Such mixture was not held a stain).
Oft in glimmering bowers and glades
He met her, and in secret shades
Of woody Ida's inmost grove,
While yet there was no fear of Jove.
Come pensive nun, devout and pure,
Sober, steadfast, and demure,
All in a robe of darkest grain,
Flowing with majestic train,
And sable stole of cypress lawn
Over thy decent shoulders drawn.
Come, but keep thy wonted state,
With even step and musing gait,
And looks commercing with the skies,
Thy rapt soul sitting in thine eyes:
There held in holy passion still,
Forget thyself to marble, till
With a sad leaden downward cast,
Thou fix them on the earth as fast.
And join with thee calm Peace and Quiet,
Spare Fast, that oft with gods doth diet,
And hears the Muses in a ring
Aye round about Jove's altar sing.

## *L'Allegro*

1 What is implied by the use of an Italian title?
2 To whom is the 'Hence' addressed? Where does this place the reader? Are there any more imperative form verbs? (Note the verb is here implied.)
3 Does 'uncouth' have an older meaning? And what does 'yclept' mean? And 'cranks'?
4 Who are all the people referred to?
5 Which abstract nouns are capitalised? Why?
6 Where does the poet write adjective/noun pairs, and where noun/adjective pairs? Why the variation?
7 What is the grammatical function of the word 'sager'?
8 Why are some words accented?
9 What kind of poetic voice do you hear?

When you feel that you have got the meaning clear, read the poem aloud and listen to its voice.

## *Il Penseroso*

1 What is implied by the use of an Italian title?
2 To whom is the 'Hence' addressed? Where does this place the reader? Are there any more imperative form verbs? Note that the verb 'Hail' is exclamatory.
3 What does 'bestead' mean?
4 Explain 'pensioners'.
5 Who are all the people referred to?
6 How are the words 'gay', 'train', 'sage' and 'hit' used?
7 What adjective/noun or noun/adjective pairs do you find noticeable and possibly characteristic of this kind of poetry?
8 Again, when you have a clear idea of the rhythm and meaning of the poem, read it aloud to hear its characteristic voice.

Now list the words that create the essential semantic field for each poem. They should contrast quite strongly. Putting aside changes of usage and meaning that have occurred with some of the words over three and a half centuries, there are factors of language use in this kind of poetry that present difficulties to modern readers. Certainly Milton is not a popular poet today; identify some of his poetic strategies that might account for this. It is not enough to say that modern readers find him 'boring'.

The two poems are sometimes likened by critics to a pair of classical paintings. How 'visual' do you find them? How many visual images, for example, do the long sentences contain?

The following parody by Joyce Johnson of Milton's style may also help you identify specific features:

'But come, due Care, and bring with thee
Good Housewif'ry and Husbandry.
In tidy habit, frugal Thrift,
Come, collect, and sort and shift.
Cast not away the scrumpled bag,
The cardboard box, the ancient mag.
Into neat sheaves the papers bind;
Thus saved, recycled and refined,
Reports of yesterday's defeats
Can be tomorrow's fairer sheets,
Where Clio, on the virgin page,
May yet record a wiser age'.

Which words have a 'Miltonic' ring, and which sound very twentieth century and incongruous?

# Poem layout

**ACTIVITY 42**

The following poems achieve a distinctly visual effect on the page through such means as punctuation, word layout and even letter arrangement. Read each poem and explain what the actual appearance of the poem contributes to understanding and appreciating the poem.

- Dickinson's *Much Madness is Divinest Sense*
- Cummings's *l(a*

Much Madness is divinest Sense—
To a discerning Eye—
Much Sense—the starkest Madness—
'Tis the Majority
In this, as All, prevail—
Assent—and you are sane—
Demur—you're straightway dangerous—
And handled with a Chain—

l(a

le
af
fa

ll

s)
one
l

iness

## *The Sick Rose by William Blake*

**ACTIVITY 43**

William Blake's poem, *The Sick Rose* has a reading age of nine years if word difficulty is assessed at face value, yet critics have long debated its interpretation. Read the poem but do not be put off by its mysteries. Read it aloud too, though on this occasion it has to be admitted that phonology is not likely to help very much.

Where do the problems lie? In identifying the rose addressed? In the adjective noun pairs? In the verb 'found out'? Do you, in the end, give up? Or can you construct a meaning? If so, what kind of a meaning is it? Fantastic? Symbolic? Botanical? Erotic?

### The Sick Rose

O Rose, thou art sick.
The invisible worm
That flies in the night
In the howling storm

Has found out thy bed
Of crimson joy,
And his dark secret love
Does thy life destroy.

# *Spelling by Margaret Atwood*

## ACTIVITY 44

The chapter began with a poet reflecting on the nature of language and ends in similar vein. Margaret Atwood's poem *Spelling*, starts in deceptively familiar territory but becomes progressively more disturbing.

Read the poem and write a running commentary noting points at which you have to stop and think.

Here are some likely questions:

1. There is a distinct thematic shift between between the first two verses, how do you connect the two?
2. What does 'mainline' mean?
3. How do you explain a 'However' between two full stops?
4. What exactly is 'the story' being returned to?
5. What exactly is the 'metaphor'?
6. Is there any reassurance in the final verse?

## Spelling

My daughter plays on the floor
with plastic letters,
red, blue & hard yellow,
learning how to spell,
spelling,
how to make spells

○

and I wonder how many women
denied themselves daughters,
closed themselves in rooms,
drew the curtains
so they could mainline words.

○

A child is not a poem,
a poem is not a child.
There is no either/or.
However.

○

I return to the story
of the woman caught in the war
& in labor, her thighs tied
together by the enemy
so she could not give birth.

○

Ancestress: the burning witch,
her mouth covered by leather
to strangle the words.

A word after a word
after a word is power.

○

At the point where language falls away
from the hot bones, at the point
where the rock breaks open and darkness
flows out of it like blood, at
the melting point of granite
when the bones know
they are hollow & the word
splits & doubles & speaks
the truth & the body
itself becomes a mouth.

This is a metaphor.

○

How do you learn to spell?
Blood, sky & the sun,
your own name first,
your first naming, your first name,
your first word.

# *Beware: do not read this poem by Ishmael Reed*

## ACTIVITY 45

To judge from poems by Robert Graves and Margaret Atwood, writing about language and life seems to lead into deep water for the one and fire and pain for the other. The last poem for you to consider is a more amusing fantasy about what happens to people who read poetry.

### beware : do not read this poem

tonite, thriller was
abt an ol woman, so vain she
surrounded herself w/
   many mirrors

it got so bad that finally she
locked herself indoors & her
whole life became the
   mirrors

one day the villagers broke
into her house, but she was too
swift for them. she disappeared
   into a mirror

each tenant who bought the house
after that, lost a loved one to
   the ol woman in the mirror :
   first a little girl
   then a young woman
   then the young woman/s husband

the hunger of this poem is legendary
it has taken in many victims
back off from this poem
it has drawn in yr feet
back off from this poem
it has drawn in yr legs
back off from this poem
it is a greedy mirror
you are into this poem. from
   the waist down
nobody can hear you can they?
this poem has had you up to here
   belch
this poem aint got no manners
you cant call out frm this poem
relax now & go w/ this poem
move & roll on to this poem
do not resist this poem
this poem has yr eyes
this poem has his head
this poem has his arms
this poem has his fingers
this poem has his fingertips

this poem is the reader & the
reader this poem

statistic: the us bureau of missing persons reports
   that in 1968 over 100,000 people disappeared
   leaving no solid clues
      nor trace      only
a space      in the lives of their friends

Read the poem and examine its unconventional elements. What do they achieve? Examine also more conventional instances of verbal art, like repetitions. What do they achieve? Is the poem entirely a joke? You could experiment with the idea of the poem itself being a consumer of readers by applying it to a scary story for children in which readers are absorbed into the world of the story, never to be seen again: *beware: do not read this story.*

# Some topics for exploration

Look at all instances of non-standard or non-existent punctuation in all the poems in this book and write an explanation of the effects achieved. What is offered that would not be there with conventional punctuation? Illustrate each point you make by a specific example.

It is a common view that poems are word paintings full of images. Poems also argue. Identify words and phrases that engage the reader in an argument: for example, the use of the word 'but'.

The opening word of a sentence has a crucial bearing on the structure of the rest of the sentence. Similarly, opening lines of a poem establish a relationship with the reader and start the poem off. Look at the opening lines of all the poems in this book and answer the question, 'How do you begin a poem?' Pay attention to title type, pronoun reference, sentence function, punctuation, concreteness, rhythm, level of formality and voice.

If you had to write an encyclopaedia entry under the heading, 'Poetic Function', what three examples (no more than one or two lines each) would you choose to illustrate language functioning poetically. Write about two hundred words, confining yourself to the poems in this book.

An extraordinarily rich area of poetic expression and language play is the modern song lyric. Choose some examples from songs with which you are familiar and examine what sorts of things the songwriters do with language that makes the lyrics memorable, moving, amusing, shocking, intriguing, clever, romantic.

# Summary

In this chapter you have explored a number of language functions evident in poetry which you should be able to recognise in other poems. They are:

- the tradition of 'musing' on life and love
- word play, deviance and breaking everyday language rules
- obscurity and ambiguity
- wordcraft and formal construction.

# 5 The Play's the Thing

## Survey

In this chapter you will look at texts that originated as playscripts or filmscripts. The texts you will look at are:

- *The Day They Shot John Lennon* by James McLure and *Educating Rita* by Willy Russell – two varieties of naturalistic dialogue
- *The Big Sleep* – a comparison of Raymond Chandler's novel with the screen adaptation
- *The Last to Go*, by Harold Pinter

## *The Day They Shot John Lennon by James McLure*

The date is 9 December, 1980, the day John Lennon was shot. Shortly after the shooting was announced, people began to gather across the street from the apartment house where Lennon lived in New York. Among them are Fran, a feminist 'looking for a relationship' and Brian who is 'in advertising'. They strike up a conversation in which Fran expresses strong political views:

**Brian:** (Impressed). Wow. You know, you're a very passionate woman
**Fran:** Well, what did you expect? Someone dumb?
**Brian:** No, it's just that women—
**Fran:** Oh brother, here we go. It's just that women what?
**Brian:** Just that women that you meet in bars—
**Fran:** Hey! You didn't meet ME in a bar! Right? Get it?
**Brian:** But you said you go to bars.
**Fran:** I go to bars. I wasn't born in a bar. Right?
**Brian:** It's just that I think you're very smart and very passionate and very attractive. And I don't meet women like that.
**Fran:** Where do you meet your 'women', Brian?
**Brian:**: Bars. I meet my women in bars.
**Fran:** Well, then maybe that's YOUR problem, Brian.

It is very difficult for a reader to resist being drawn into a conversation such as this. It creates the illusion of an everyday situation; the language is easy and can be read at high speed; above all, it is that most familiar language mode, casual chat. But in fact, the whole scene is verbal art, resembling aspects of real conversation yet originating inside a writer's head, namely James McLure's.

In examinations, many candidates appear to forget this and treat a playscript as though it were a transcript. True, features such as 'Right?' and 'Well, . . .' can be given the conversation analysis treatment but only if it is understood that these are the choices of James McLure and given to Fran to speak.

## *Educating Rita by Willy Russell*

### ACTIVITY 46

The following excerpt comes from Willy Russell's, *Educating Rita.*

Frank is a lecturer in English literature in a university in the North of England. Not the happiest of men, he drinks too much and is hard up. He has agreed to take on an Open University student, Rita, a hairdresser with very little previous education but who is as bright as a button. As the play develops they have a profound effect on each other.

The excerpt comes from the opening scene of the play. Read the scene and explain how the writer uses ways in which people talk to each other to depict characters and the relationship between them.

As the scene below begins, Frank is in his office on the phone with his wife. They are arguing about his drinking and his having forgotten to tell her he'd be working late (the meal she prepared has burned). There is a knock at the door.

**Frank**: Look, I'll have to go. . . . There's someone at the door. . . . Yes, yes I promise. . . . Just a couple of pints. . . . Four. . . .

(*There is another knock at the door.*)

(*Calling in the direction of the door.*) Come in! (*He continues on the telephone.*) Yes. . . . All right . . . Yes. . . . Bye, bye. . . . (*He replaces the receiver.*) Yes, that's it, you just pop off and put your head in the oven. (*Shouting*) Come in! Come in!

(*The door swings open revealing* RITA.)

**Rita:** (*From the doorway.*) I'm comin' in, aren't I? It's that stupid bleedin' handle on the door. You wanna get it fixed! (*She comes into the room.*)

**Frank**: (*Staring, slightly confused.*) Erm—yes, I suppose I always mean to . . .

**Rita:** (*Going to the chair by the desk and dumping her bag.*) Well that's no good, always meanin' to, is it? Y' should get on with it; one of these days you'll be shoutin' "Come in" an' it'll go on forever because the poor sod on the other side won't be *able* to get in. An' you won't be able to get out.

(FRANK *stares at* RITA *who stands by the desk.*)

**Frank**: You are?

**Rita:** What am I?

**Frank**: Pardon?

**Rita:** What?

**Frank**: (*Looking for the admission papers.*) Now you are?

**Rita:** I'm a what?

(FRANK *looks up and then returns to the papers as* RITA *goes to hang her coat on the door hooks.*)

(*Noticing the picture.*) That's a nice picture, isn't it? (*She goes up to it.*)

**Frank:** Erm—yes, I suppose it is—nice . . .
**Rita:** (*Studying the picture.*) It's very erotic.
**Frank:** (*Looking up.*) Actually I don't think I've looked at it for about ten years, but yes, I suppose it is.
**Rita:** There's no suppose about it. Look at those tits.

(*He coughs and goes back to looking for the admission paper.*)

Is it supposed to be erotic? I mean when he painted it do y' think he wanted to turn people on?

**Frank:** Erm—probably.
**Rita:** I'll bet he did y' know. Y' don't paint pictures like that just so that people can admire the brush strokes, do y'?
**Frank:** (*Giving a short laugh.*) No—no—you're probably right.
**Rita:** This was the pornography of its day, wasn't it? It's sort of like *Men Only*, isn't it? But in those days they had to pretend it wasn't erotic so they made it religious, didn't they? Do *you* think it's erotic?
**Frank:** (*Taking a look.*) I think it's very beautiful.
**Rita:** I didn't ask y' if it was beautiful.
**Frank:** But the term "beautiful" covers the many feelings I have about that picture, including the feeling that, yes, it is erotic.
**Rita:** (*Coming back to the desk.*) D' y' get a lot like me?
**Frank:** Pardon?
**Rita:** Do you get a lot of students like me?
**Frank:** Not exactly, no . . .
**Rita:** I was dead surprised when they took me. I don't suppose they would have done if it'd been a proper university. The Open University's different though, isn't it?
**Frank:** I've—erm—not had much more experience of it than you. This is the first O.U. work I've done.
**Rita:** D' y' need the money?
**Frank:** I do as a matter of fact.
**Rita:** It's terrible these days, the money, isn't it? With the inflation an' that. You work for the ordinary university, don't y'? With the real students. The Open University's different, isn't it?
**Frank:** It's supposed to embrace a more comprehensive studentship, yes.
**Rita:** (*Inspecting a bookcase.*) Degrees for dishwashers.
**Frank:** Would you—erm—would you like to sit down?
**Rita:** No! Can I smoke? (*She goes to her bag and rummages in it.*)
**Frank:** Tobacco?
**Rita:** Yeh. (*She half-laughs.*) Was that a joke? (*She takes out a packet of cigarettes and a lighter.*) Here—d' y' want one? (*She takes out two cigarettes and dumps the packet on the desk.*)
**Frank:** (*After a pause.*) Ah—I'd love one.
**Rita:** Well, have one.
**Frank:** (*After a pause.*) I—don't smoke—I made a promise not to smoke.
**Rita:** Well, I won't tell anyone.
**Frank:** Promise?

(*As* FRANK *goes to take the cigarette* RITA *whips it from his reach.*)

**Rita:** (*Doing a Brownie salute.*) On my oath as an ex Brownie. (*She gives him the cigarette.*) I hate smokin' on me own. An' everyone seems to have packed up these days. (*She lights the cigarettes.*) They're all afraid of gettin' cancer.

(FRANK *looks dubiously at his cigarette.*)

But they're all cowards.

**Frank:** Are they?
**Rita:** You've got to challenge death an' disease. I read this poem about fightin' death . . .
**Frank:** Ah—Dylan Thomas . . .
**Rita:** No. Roger McGough. It was about this old man who runs away from hospital an' goes out on the ale. He gets pissed an' stands in the street shoutin' an' challengin' death to come out an' fight. It's dead good.
**Frank:** Yes. I don't think I know the actual piece you mean . . .
**Rita:** I'll bring y' the book—it's great.
**Frank:** Thank you.
**Rita:** You probably won't think it's any good.

**Frank:** Why?
**Rita:** It's the sort of poetry you can understand.
**Frank:** Ah. I see.

(RITA *begins looking idly round the room.*)

Can I offer you a drink?

**Rita:** What of?
**Frank:** Scotch?
**Rita:** (*Going to the bookcase U.R.*) Y' wanna be careful with that stuff, it kills y' brain cells.
**Frank:** But you'll have one? (*He gets up and goes to the small table.*)
**Rita:** All right. It'll probably have a job findin' my brain.
**Frank:** (*Pouring the drinks.*) Water?
**Rita:** (*Looking at the bookcase.*) Yeh, all right. (*She takes a copy of "Howards End" from the shelf.*) What's this like?

(FRANK *goes over to* RITA, *looks at the title of the book and then goes back to the drinks.*)

**Frank:** *Howards End*?
**Rita:** Yeh. It sounds filthy, doesn't it? E. M. Foster.
**Frank:** Forster.
**Rita:** Oh yeh. What's it like?
**Frank:** Borrow it. Read it.
**Rita:** Ta. I'll look after it. (*She moves back towards the desk.*) If I pack the course in I'll post it to y'.

(FRANK *comes to the desk with the drinks.*)

**Frank:** (*Handing her the mug.*) Pack it in? Why should you do that?

(RITA *puts her drink down on the desk and puts the copy of "Howards End" in her bag.*)

**Rita:** I just might. I might decide it was a soft idea.
**Frank:** (*Looking at her.*) Mm. Cheers. If—erm—if you're already contemplating "packing it in," why did you enroll in the first place?
**Rita:** Because I wanna know.
**Frank:** What do you want to know?
**Rita:** Everything.
**Frank:** Everything? That's rather a lot, isn't it? Where would you like to start?
**Rita:** Well, I'm a student now, aren't I? I'll have to do exams, won't I?
**Frank:** Yes. Eventually.
**Rita:** I'll have to learn about it all, won' I? Yeh. It's like y' sit there, don't y', watchin' the ballet or the opera on the telly an'—an' y' call it rubbish cos that's what it looks like? Cos y' don't understand. So y' switch it off an' say, that's fuckin' rubbish.
**Frank:** Do you?
**Rita:** I do. But I don't want to. I wanna see. Y' don't mind me swearin', do y'?
**Frank:** Not at all.
**Rita:** Do you swear?
**Frank:** Never stop.
**Rita:** See, the educated classes know it's only words, don't they? It's only the masses who don't understand. I do it to shock them sometimes. Y' know when I'm in the hairdresser's—that's where I work—I'll say somethin' like, "Oh, I'm really fucked," y' know, dead loud. It doesn't half cause a fuss.
**Frank:** Yes—I'm sure . . .
**Rita:** But it doesn't cause any sort of fuss with educated people, does it? Cos they know it's only words and they don't worry. But these stuck-up idiots I meet, they think they're royalty just cos they don't swear; an' I wouldn't mind but it's the aristocracy that swears more than anyone, isn't it? They're effin' an' blindin' all day long. It's all "Pass me the fackin' grouse" with them, isn't it? But y' can't tell them that round our way. It's not their fault; they can't help it. (*She goes to the window and looks out.*) But sometimes I hate them. God, what's it like to be free?
**Frank:** Ah. Now there's a question. Will you have another drink? (*He goes to the small table.*)
**Rita:** (*Shaking her head.*) If I'd got some other tutor I wouldn't have stayed.
**Frank:** (*Pouring himself a drink.*) What sort of other tutor?
**Rita:** Y' know, someone who objected to swearin'.
**Frank:** How did you know I wouldn't object?

**Rita:** I didn't. I was just testin' y'.
**Frank:** (*Coming back to the desk and looking at her.*) Yes. You're doing rather a lot of that, aren't you?
**Rita:** That's what I do. Y' know, when I'm nervous.
**Frank:** (*Sitting in the swivel chair.*) And how am I scoring so far?
**Rita:** Very good, ten out of ten go to the top of the class an' collect a gold star. I love this room. I love that window. Do you like it?
**Frank:** What?
**Rita:** The window.
**Frank:** I don't often consider it actually. I sometimes get an urge to throw something through it.
**Rita:** What?
**Frank:** A student usually.
**Rita:** (*Smiling.*) You're bleedin' mad you, aren't y'?
**Frank:** Probably.

(*Pause.*)

**Rita:** Aren't you supposed to be interviewin' me?
**Frank:** (*Looking at the drink.*) Do I need to?
**Rita:** I talk too much, don't I? I know I talk a lot. I don't at home. I hardly ever talk when I'm there. But I don't often get the chance to talk to someone like you; to talk at you. D' y' mind?
**Frank:** Would you be at all bothered if I did?

(*She shakes her head and then turns it into a nod.*)

I don't mind. (*He takes a sip of his drink.*)

**Rita:** What does assonance mean?
**Frank:** (*Half-spluttering.*) What? (*He gives a short laugh.*)
**Rita:** Don't laugh at me.
**Frank:** No. Erm—assonance. Well, it's a form of rhyme. What's a—what's an example—erm—? Do you know Yeats?
**Rita:** The wine lodge?
**Frank:** Yeats the poet.
**Rita:** No.
**Frank:** Oh. Well—there's a Yeats poem, called *The Wild Swans at Coole*. In it he rhymes the sword "swan" with the word "stone." There, you see, an example of assonance.
**Rita:** Oh. It means gettin' the rhyme wrong.
**Frank:** (*Looking at her and laughing.*) I've never really looked at it like that. But yes, yes you could say it means getting the rhyme wrong; but purposefully, in order to achieve a certain effect.
**Rita:** Oh. (*There is a pause and she wanders round.*) There's loads I don't know.
**Frank:** And you want to know everything?
**Rita:** Yeh.

(FRANK *nods and then takes her admission paper from his desk and looks at it.*)

**Frank:** What's your name?
**Rita:** (*Moving towards the bookcase.*) Rita.
**Frank:** (*Looking at the paper.*) Rita. Mm. It says here Mrs. S. White.

(RITA *goes to the right of* FRANK, *takes a pencil, leans over and scratches out the initial "S."*)

**Rita:** That's "S" for Susan. It's just me real name. I've changed it to Rita, though. I'm not a Susan anymore. I've called meself Rita—y' know, after Rita Mae Brown.
**Frank:** Who?
**Rita:** Y' know, Rita Mae Brown who wrote *Rubyfruit Jungle*? Haven't y' read it? It's a fantastic book. D' y' wanna lend it?
**Frank:** I'd—erm—I'd be very interested.
**Rita:** All right.

(RITA *gets a copy of "Rubyfruit Jungle" from her bag and gives it to* FRANK. *He turns it over and reads the blurb on the back cover.*)

What's your name?

**Frank:** Frank.
**Rita:** Oh. Not after Frank Harris?

**Frank**: Not after Frank anyone.
**Rita**: Maybe y' parents named y' after the quality. (*She sits in the chair by the desk.*)

(FRANK *puts down "Rubyfruit Jungle."*)

Y' know Frank, Frank Ness. Elliot's brother.

**Frank**: What?
**Rita**: I'm sorry—it was a joke. Y' know, Frank Ness, Elliot's brother.
**Frank**: (*Bemused.*) Ah.
**Rita**: You've still not got it, have y'? Elliot Ness—y' know, the famous Chicago copper who caught Al Capone.
**Frank**: Ah. When you said Elliot I assumed you meant T. S. Eliot.
**Rita**: Have you read his stuff?
**Frank**: Yes.
**Rita**: All of it?
**Frank**: Every last syllable.
**Rita**: (*Impressed.*) Honest? I couldn't even get through one poem. I tried to read this thing he wrote called *J. Arthur Prufrock*; I couldn't finish it.
**Frank**: *J. Alfred*.
**Rita**: What?
**Frank**: I think you'll find it was *J. Alfred Prufrock*, Rita. J. Arthur is something else altogether.
**Rita**: Oh yeh. I never thought of that. I've not half got a lot to learn, haven't I?
**Frank**: (*Looking at her paper.*) You're a ladies' hairdresser?
**Rita**: Yeh.
**Frank**: Are you good at it?
**Rita**: (*Getting up and wandering around.*) I am when I wanna be. Most of the time I don't want to though. They get on me nerves.
**Frank**: Who?
**Rita**: The women. They never tell y' things that matter. Like, y' know, doin' a perm, well y' can't use a strong perm lotion on a head that's been bleached with certain sorts of cheap bleach. It makes all the hair break off. But at least once a month I'll get a customer in for a perm who'll swear to God that she's not had any bleach on; an' I can tell, I mean I can see it. So y'go ahead an' do the perm an' she comes out the drier with half an inch of stubble.
**Frank**: And what do you do about it?
**Rita**: Try and sell them a wig.
**Frank**: My God.
**Rita**: Women who want their hair doin', they won't stop at anythin', y' know. Even the pensioners are like that, y' know; a pensioner'll come in an' she won't tell y' that she's got a hearin' aid: so y' start cuttin' don't y'? Next thing—snip—another granny deaf for a fortnight. I'm always cuttin' hearin' aid cords. An' ear lobes.
**Frank**: You sound like something of a liability.
**Rita**: I am. But they expect too much. They walk in the hairdresser's an' an hour later they wanna walk out a different person. I tell them I'm a hairdresser, not a plastic surgeon. It's worse when there's a fad on, y' know like Farrah Fawcett Majors.
**Frank**: Who?
**Rita**: Far-rah Fawcett Majors. Y'know, she used to be with *Charlie's Angels*.

(FRANK *remains blank.*)

It's a telly programme on ITV.

**Frank**: Ah.
**Rita**: (*Wandering towards the door.*) You wouldn't watch ITV though, would y'? It's all BBC with you, isn't it?
**Frank**: Well, I must confess . . .
**Rita**: It's all right, I know. Soon as I walked in here I said to meself, "Y' can tell he's a *Flora* man."
**Frank**: A what?
**Rita**: A *Flora* man.
**Frank**: Flora? Flowers?
**Rita**: (*Coming back to the desk.*) No, *Flora*, the bleedin' margarine, no cholesterol; it's for people like you who eat pebble-dashed bread, y' know the bread, with little hard bits in it, just like pebble-dashin'.

**Frank**: (*Realizing and smiling*.) Ah—pebble-dashed bread.
**Rita:** Quick? He's like lightenin'. But these women, you see, they come to the hairdresser's cos they wanna be changed. But if you want to change y' have to do it from the inside, don't y'? Know like I'm doin'. Do y' think I'll be able to do it?
**Frank**: Well, it really depends on you, on how committed you are. Are you sure that you're absolutely serious about wanting to learn?
**Rita:** I'm dead serious. Look, I know I take the piss an' that but I'm dead serious really. I take the piss because I'm not, y' know, confident like, but I wanna be, honest.

**COMMENTARY**

A quick scan reveals that language itself is a frequent topic throughout the conversation:

- swearing
- assonance
- name changing
- reading interests
- confused names.

Speech styles are noticeably contrasted, Frank's speech more educated and more succinct, Rita's, more chatty and closer to dialectal idioms (Liverpudlian).

In this scene, Rita introduces the topics, sometimes prompted by questions from Frank. Excluding tag questions, Frank asks 21 questions, Rita, 18. There are occasions when a question is answered by another question:

**Rita**: Aren't you supposed to be interviewin' me?
**Frank**: Do I need to?

and

**Rita**: D'y' mind?
**Frank**: Would you be at all bothered if I did?

Clearly in an interview you would expect lots of questions but the types of questions, and their topics also delineate character as much as the answers given. Rita, for example, veers between direct, personal questions, such as, 'Do you swear?' and 'Have you read this stuff?' and sudden, academic questions like, 'What does assonance mean?' Notice that one of her questions combines the two in a rhetorical vein: 'God, what's it like to be free?'

Frank's questions are prompted partly by interview routine but also by growing interest in Rita. In general the talk is characterised by a spirit of friendly candour but some guardedness. There's a certain amount of verbal swordplay (compare this with the excerpts from *The Importance of Being Earnest* and *Romeo and Juliet*). Cultural differences are very apparent from the outset yet Russell gradually reveals that intellectually the two characters are much closer in terms of sharpness and honesty. Toward the end, Russell's own comment on this is marked in italics as a stage direction:

**Frank**: (*Realising and smiling*) Ah – pebble-dashed bread.

Frank is already beginning to learn appreciatively from his student. Rita's response is good humouredly sarcastic: 'Quick? He's like lightenin'.

By a series of misunderstandings and personal undercurrents, Russell brings the scene to a 'serious' juncture in which Rita summarises herself in her own idiom but with something of Frank's succinctness: 'Look, I know I take the piss an' that but I'm dead serious really'. Note a good playwright's ear for what people actually say: 'an' that' is a very popular tag, 'dead' a very popular adverb.

Even though the dialogue here may seem very naturalistic it is still verbal art, as carefully constructed for effects as that of Shakespeare or Wilde, both of whom may seem much less naturalistic partly because of the distance in time between them and modern readers or playgoers.

Throughout the scene, different 'audiences' are addressed by the playwright. There are the actors playing Frank and Rita who need to know what to say but who are also given instructions as to movement and manner; the references to a small table, swivel chair and desk, for example, address the stage designer; other references address, implicitly the properties manager.

Ultimately, everything addresses the director for its complete realisation on the stage for the benefit of the final audience, the theatregoers. These are the linguistic necessities of drama texts.

A literary scholar, A. C. Bradley (1851–1935), introduced the idea of the 'theatre of the mind' to describe the experience of reading a playscript as opposed to attending a performance.

There is no doubt that much can be imagined and enjoyed in reading a playscript but it is just as important linguistically to keep performance in mind, as it is theatrically. There are codes at work between theatre audiences and play performances, that determine appropriate ranges of expression, variations in style, dialect and address, and use of body language. Audiences expect performances to conform to established norms of stage behaviour; variations are always undertaken at some risk. Another term for expectations is 'structures'. These are combinations of features that come to mind unbidden but which exist in a culture and automatically construct character types and familiar storylines. When they become over familiar, and 'unreal' they are called stereotypes. Most actors dread becoming typecast.

Russell's characters are not stereotypes; the vitality of the lines they are given to speak prevents that. It would be easy to stereotype the characters for another play: world weary, boozing, low paid, ironical but charming lecturer meets swearing, chirpy, working class hairdresser with a mind of her own and much more common sense. The point is that Willy Russell perceived them first as an authentic element in English life, and gave them a voice.

Of many issues deserving comment in this excerpt is the love interest that any audience brings to a scene such as this. Literature isn't created just out of words on the page but also out of shared imaginings and preoccupations that have been in the culture since time immemorial. Myths of heroes and lovers, legends of good and bad fortune, family sagas, tales of blood and revenge, contrasts of good and evil are familiar to everybody. It is not too much of an exaggeration to say that literature is concerned with three things: love, death and money. It is not difficult to find one or all of these running through the excerpts so far so long as you take money as a symbol for status as well as material wealth.

Will Frank and Rita fall in love? Have they already done so? Both questions subtly affect performance, not only of the line, 'Because – I think you're marvellous' (notice the pause specifically marked by Russell), but also of the stage direction, 'He nods and looks at her. She becomes uncomfortable'.

**ACTIVITY 47**

The issue of performance needs further exploration. It is especially important where the actual written texts remain the same from one performance to another.

The word 'performance' is a familiar one in linguistics in the sense of specific uses of language by individuals. Performance here is distinguished from 'competence' which is the total repertoire, the full potential, of a language from which 'performers' (that is language users), draw their material at any given time. Performance is not just a matter for theatrical or cinematic texts, it is also a matter for any context in which speakers perform scripted speech.

Think about the following occasions: public readings of holy scriptures; news readings; poetry readings; the Queen's speech; religious or lay ceremonies; court room formalities; nursery rhymes and stories read to young children. Choose two of these and list what you would consider norms of speech style, or performance, for each one. Suggest also acceptable and unacceptable variations.

As you look at norms and permissible variations, you are likely to observe a number of social regulations placed on performance and a number of features audiences expect.

Next, compare the Russell excerpt with either the Shakespeare or the Wilde excerpt. What performance factors do they have in common? What variations in style are necessary, and why?

## *The Big Sleep: Screenplay and novel*

**ACTIVITY 48**

The next excerpt is taken from a filmscript of the classic film noir, *The Big Sleep.* The story was originally written by Raymond Chandler; the film version is an adaptation of his novel by William Faulkner, Leigh Brackett and Jules Furthman. Notice that the screenplay was written by three writers and that the realisation of the film depended upon many more people.

Philip Marlowe, a private eye, has been hired by a wealthy invalid to investigate and deal with blackmail and gambling scandals affecting his two daughters, Vivian and Carmel. The plot line of the film adaptation becomes so tortuous that even the director, Howard Hawks, remarked that he 'never figured out what was going on'. First read the following excerpt which is the scene in the novel upon which the screenplay was based. Then read the scene in the film. After witnessing some murderous goings-on during a stake-out the night before, Marlowe turns up at his office to find Vivian waiting for him.

Read the excerpt noting the following:

1 What is the style of conversation?
2 Are there any elements that mark it as a screenplay?
3 Are there any implied meanings or undercurrents?
4 What changes have been made to the scene as described in the novel?

She wore brownish speckled tweeds, a mannish shirt and tie, hand-carved walking shoes. Her stockings were just as sheer as the day before, but she wasn't showing as much of her legs. Her black hair was glossy under a brown Robin Hood hat that might have cost fifty dollars and looked as if you could have made it with one hand out of a desk blotter.

'Well, you *do* get up,' she said, wrinkling her nose at the faded red settee, the two odd semi-easy chairs, the net curtains that needed laundering and the boy's size library table with the venerable magazines on it to give the place a professional touch. 'I was beginning to think perhaps you worked in bed, like Marcel Proust.'

'Who's he?' I put a cigarette in my mouth and stared at her. She looked a little pale and strained, but she looked like a girl who could function under a strain.

'A French writer, a connoisseur in degenerates. You wouldn't know him.'

'Tut, tut,' I said. 'Come into my boudoir.'

She stood up and said: 'We didn't get along very well yesterday. Perhaps I was rude.'

'We were both rude,' I said. I unlocked the communicating door and held it for her. We went into the rest of my suite, which contained a rust-red carpet, not very young, five green filing cases, three of them full of California climate, an advertising calendar showing the Quins rolling around on a sky-blue floor, in pink dresses, with seal-brown hair and sharp black eyes as large as mammoth prunes. There were three near-walnut chairs, the usual desk with the usual blotter, pen set, ashtray and telephone, and the usual squeaky swivel chair behind it.

'You don't put on much of a front,' she said, sitting down at the customer's side of the desk.

I went over to the mail slot and picked up six envelopes, two letters and four pieces of advertising matter. I hung my hat on the telephone and sat down.

'Neither do the Pinkertons,' I said. 'You can't make much money at this trade, if you're honest. If you have a front, you're making money – or expect to.'

'Oh – are you honest?' she asked and opened her bag. She picked a cigarette out of a French enamel case, lit it with a pocket lighter, dropped case and lighter back into the bag and left the bag open.

'Painfully.'

'How did you ever get into this slimy kind of business then?'

'How did you come to marry a bootlegger?'

'My God, let's not start quarrelling again. I've been trying to get you on the phone all morning. Here and at your apartment.'

'About Owen?'

Her face tightened sharply. Her voice was soft. 'Poor Owen,' she said. 'So you know about that.'

'ADA's man took me down to Lido. He thought I might know something about it. But he knew much more than I did. He knew Owen wanted to marry your sister – once.'

She puffed silently at her cigarette and considered me with steady black eyes. 'Perhaps it wouldn't have been a bad idea,' she said quietly. 'He was in love with her. We don't find much of that in our circle.'

'He had a police record.'

She shrugged. She said negligently: 'He didn't know the right people. That's all a police record means in this rotten crime-ridden country.'

'I wouldn't go that far.'

She peeled her right glove off and bit her index finger at the first joint, looking at me with steady eyes. 'I didn't come to see you about Owen. Do you feel yet that you can tell me what my father wanted to see you about?'

'Not without his permission.'

'Was it about Carmen?'

'I can't even say that.' I finished filling a pipe and put a match to it. She watched the smoke for a moment. Then her hand went into her open bag and came out with a thick white envelope. She tossed it across the desk.

'You'd better look at it anyway,' she said.

I picked it up. The address was typewritten to Mrs Vivian Regan, 3765 Alta Brea Crescent, West Hollywood.

Delivery had been by messenger service and the office stamp showed 8.35 a.m. as the time out. I opened the envelope and drew out the shiny 4¼ by 3¼ photo that was all there was inside.

It was Carmen sitting in Geiger's high-backed teakwood chair on the dais, in her earrings and her birthday suit. Her eyes looked even a little crazier than as I remembered them. The back of the photo was blank. I put it back in the envelope.

'How much do they want?' I asked.

'Five thousand – for the negative and the rest of the prints. The deal has to be closed to-night, or they give the stuff to some scandal sheet.'

'The demand came how?'

'A woman telephoned me, about half an hour after this thing was delivered.'

'There's nothing in the scandal sheet angle. Juries convict without leaving the box on that stuff nowadays. What else is there?'

'Does there have to be something else?'

'Yes.'

She stared at me, a little puzzled. 'There is. The woman said there was a police jam connected with it and I'd better lay it on the line fast, or I'd be talking to my little sister through a wire screen.'

'Better,' I said. 'What kind of jam?'

'I don't know.'

'Where is Carmen now?'

'She's at home. She was sick last night. She's still in bed, I think.'

'Did she go out last night?'

'No. I was out, but the servants say she wasn't. I was down at Las Olindas, playing roulette at Eddie Mars's Cypress Club. I lost my shirt.'

'So you like roulette. You would.'

She crossed her legs and lit another cigarette. 'Yes. I like roulette. All the Sternwoods like losing games, like roulette and marrying men that walk out on them and riding steeplechases at fifty-eight years old and being rolled on by a jumper and crippled for life. The Sternwoods have money. All it has bought them is a rain cheque.'

'What was Owen doing last night with your car?'

'Nobody knows. He took it without permission. We always let him take a car on his night off, but last night wasn't his night off.' She made a wry mouth. 'Do you think—?'

'He knew about this nude photograph? How would I be able to say? I don't rule him out. Can you get five thousand in cash right away?'

'Not unless I tell Dad – or borrow it. I could probably borrow it from Eddie Mars. He ought to be generous with me, Heaven knows.'

'Better try that. You may need it in a hurry.'

She leaned back and hung an arm over the back of the chair. 'How about telling the police?'

'It's a good idea. But you won't do it.'

'Won't I?'

'No. You have to protect your father and your sister. You don't know what the police might turn up. It might be something they couldn't sit on. Though they usually try in blackmail cases.'

'Can you do anything?'

'I think I can. But I can't tell you why or how.'

'I like you,' she said suddenly. 'You believe in miracles. Would you have a drink in the office?'

I unlocked my deep drawer and got out my office bottle and two pony glasses. I filled them and we drank. She snapped her bag shut and pushed her chair back.

'I'll get the five grand,' she said. 'I've been a good customer of Eddie Mars. There's another reason why he should be nice to me, which you may not know.' She gave me one of those smiles the lips have forgotten before they reach the eyes. 'Eddie's blonde wife is the lady Rusty ran away with.'

I didn't say anything. She stared tightly at me and added: 'That doesn't interest you?'

'It ought to make it easier to find him – if I was looking for him. You don't think he's in this mess, do you?'

She pushed her empty glass at me. 'Give me another drink. You're the hardest guy to get anything out of. You don't even move your ears.'

I filled the little glass. 'You've got all you wanted out of me – a pretty good idea I'm not looking for your husband.'

She put the drink down very quickly. It made her gasp – or gave her an opportunity to gasp. She let a breath out slowly.

'Rusty was no crook. If he had been, it wouldn't have been for nickels. He carried fifteen thousand dollars, in bills. He called it his mad money. He had it when I married him and he had it when he left me. No – Rusty's not in on any cheap blackmail racket.'

She reached for the envelope and stood up. 'I'll keep in touch with you,' I said. 'If you want to leave me a message, the phone girl at my apartment house will take care of it.'

We walked over to the door. Tapping the white envelope against her knuckles, she said: 'You still feel you can't tell me what Dad—'

'I'd have to see him first.'

She took the photo out and stood looking at it, just inside the door. 'She has a beautiful little body, hasn't she?'

'Uh-huh.'

She leaned a little towards me. 'You ought to see mine,' she said gravely.

'Can it be arranged?'

She laughed suddenly and sharply and went half-way through the door, then turned her head to say coolly: 'You're as cold-blooded a beast as I ever met, Marlowe. Or can I call you Phil?'

'Sure.'

'You can call me Vivian.'

'Thanks, Mrs Regan.'

'Oh, go to hell, Marlowe.' She went on out and didn't look back.

## (ii)

INTERIOR BUILDING—HALLWAY—AT MARLOWE'S OFFICE DOOR

MARLOWE opens the door, which has PHILIP MARLOWE in gilt letters on the upper glass.

INTERIOR MARLOWE'S OFFICE—THE WAITING ROOM

A small room, cheaply furnished, with a closed door in one wall. VIVIAN sits waiting for him, beautifully but simply dressed, quite at ease. She seems in a better humor this morning, smiling at the surprised MARLOWE.

**VIVIAN:** Well, you *do* exist, after all. I'd begun to think I dreamed you out of a bottle of bad gin. (*with underlying hint of seriousness*) I've been trying to get you on the phone all morning.

**MARLOWE:** You can insult me just as well face to face. I don't bite—much.

**VIVIAN:** (*apologetically*) I was rather rude.

**MARLOWE:** (*smiling*) An apology from a Sternwood? (*unlocking the connecting door, holding it for her*) Come into my boudoir.

INTERIOR MARLOWE'S OFFICE

Like the waiting room, it's shabby and not large. The usual desk, chairs, and filing cabinets.

**VIVIAN:** (*sitting*) You don't put on much of a front.

**MARLOWE:** You can't make much money at this trade, if you're honest. If you have a front, you're making money—or expect to.

**VIVIAN:** Oh—are you honest?

**MARLOWE:** Painfully.

**VIVIAN:** (*taking out a cigarette*) How did you get into this slimy business, then?

**MARLOWE:** (*giving her a look as he lights it for her*) Because people like you pay good money to have the slime cleaned up.

She looks away from him angry but not able to say anything.

MARLOWE SITS DOWN BEHIND THE DESK.

**MARLOWE:** What did you want to see me about? Taylor?

**VIVIAN:** (*softly*) Poor Owen. So you know about that.

**MARLOWE:** A.D.A.'s man took me down to Lido. Turned out he knew more about it than I did. He knew Owen Taylor wanted to marry your sister—once.

**VIVIAN:** (*quietly*) Perhaps it wouldn't have been a bad idea. He was in love with her. We don't find much of that in our circle. . . . (*changing her tone*) But I didn't come here to see you about Owen. Do you feel yet that you can tell me what my father wants you to do?

**MARLOWE:** Not without his permission.

**VIVIAN:** Was it about Carmen?

**MARLOWE:** I can't even say that.

VIVIAN watches him for a moment, then gives in. She takes a thick white envelope from her bag and tosses it on the desk.

**VIVIAN:** You'd better look at this anyway.

MARLOWE examines the envelope.

**VIVIAN:** A messenger brought it this morning.

**MARLOWE:** Eight-thirty-five it says—for you or your father.

He opens the envelope, takes out a medium-sized photograph. We do not see the subject of the picture, but MARLOWE's reaction is significant. He whistles softly.

**MARLOWE:** So that's what Carmen looks like! (*to* VIVIAN) How much do they want for this?

**VIVIAN:** Five thousand—for the negative and the rest of the prints. The deal has to be closed tonight, or they give the picture to some scandal sheet.

**MARLOWE:** The demand came how?

**VIVIAN:** A woman telephoned me, shortly after this thing was delivered.

**MARLOWE:** There's nothing in the scandal sheet angle. Juries convict on that racket without leaving the box. What else is there?

**VIVIAN:** Does there have to be something else?

MARLOWE nods—his face is uncompromising.

**VIVIAN:** (*giving in again*) The woman said there was a police jam connected with it, and I'd better lay it on the line fast or I'd be talking to my little sister through a wire screen.

**MARLOWE:** (*deadpan, nodding*) What kind of a jam?

**VIVIAN:** I don't know.

**MARLOWE:** Where's Carmen now?

**VIVIAN:** She's at home—still in bed, I think. She was sick last night.

**MARLOWE:** She go out at all?

**VIVIAN:** The servants say she didn't. I was up at Las Olindas across the state line playing roulette at Eddie Mars's Cypress Club. I lost my shirt. (*taking another cigarette—laughing wryly*)

**MARLOWE:** (*getting up to hold the match for her*) So you like roulette. You would.

**VIVIAN:** Yes, the Sternwoods all like losing games. The Sternwoods can afford to. The Sternwoods have money. (*bitterly*) All it's bought them is a raincheck.

**MARLOWE:** What was Owen doing with your car last night?

**VIVIAN:** Nobody knows. He took it without permission. Do you think . . .?

**MARLOWE:** He knew about this photo? (*shrugging*) I don't rule him out. . . . Can you get five thousand in cash right away?

**VIVIAN:** I can borrow it—probably from Eddie Mars. (*sardonically*) There's a bond between us, you see. Shawn Regan ran away with Eddie's blonde wife.

**MARLOWE:** (*turning away—leaving a pause*) You may need the money in a hurry.

**VIVIAN:** How about telling the police?

**MARLOWE:** You know better than that. The police might turn up something they couldn't sit on—and then where would the Sternwoods be? (*after a pause*) How was it left?

**VIVIAN:** The woman said she'd call me back with instructions at five.

**MARLOWE:** Okay—call me here as soon as you've heard from her.

**VIVIAN:** Can you do anything?

**MARLOWE:** I think so. But I can't tell you how—or why.

**VIVIAN:** I like you. You believe in miracles.

**MARLOWE:** (*laughing*) I believe in people believing they're smarter than they are—if that's a miracle. Have a drink?

He reaches down into the desk drawer.

**VIVIAN:** I'll have two drinks.

MARLOWE grins at her. He comes up with a bottle and two glasses, fills them, and takes one to her. They salute, start to drink and find that their eyes have met over the glass rims and refuse to come apart. VIVIAN breaks it, not because she is shy or coy, but because suddenly there is a sadness in her face. Her gaze drops briefly, then returns to MARLOWE, clear, steady, and sad.

**VIVIAN:** You're a lot like Shawn Regan.

MARLOWE looks at her, almost with tenderness and understanding.

**MARLOWE:** You want to tell me now or later?

**VIVIAN:** What?

**MARLOWE:** What you're so anxious to find out.

**VIVIAN:** It couldn't be—you.

**MARLOWE:** Let's do one thing at a time.

**VIVIAN:** (*rising*) I think we've done enough for one day....

**MARLOWE:** (*gently*) Want that other drink?

**VIVIAN:** (*going toward door*) No....

MARLOWE sets his glass down on the desk and picks up the envelope.

**MARLOWE:** You forgot this ...

She turns by the door as he approaches, holding out her hand for the envelope. MARLOWE gives it to her, but doesn't let go of it.

They are not thinking about the envelope. Slowly he bends to her—she leans back against the wall, her lips parted, her eyes soft, misted with tears. MARLOWE's mouth covers hers. Presently they break—VIVIAN puts her hand on MARLOWE's cheek.

**VIVIAN:** (*softly*) Your face is like Shawn's too—clean and thin, with hard bones under it ...

She turns, neither slowly nor fast, away from him, opens the door, and goes out.

## ACTIVITY 50

Look at *Miss Brill* again. Is it filmable? If you think it is, write a screenplay for the opening scene including arrival at the park, or write the section leading up to and including the scene with the young couple. There are a number of literary possibilities you will need to consider before deciding on your narrative technique – all of them linguistic.

1 Will you use voice-over? If so, where and when?
2 Will you direct instructions to the actors?
3 How will you direct the camera(s)?
4 Will Miss Brill actually appear or will she in effect be the camera?
5 How will you suggest mood?

In the case of *The Big Sleep*, you could compare your approach with the actual film. Here you are entirely on your own. Knowing what to do with the camera to catch the essence of Katherine Mansfield's narrative style depends very much on your understanding of how she uses language to express both the narrator's and Miss Brill's thoughts.

## COMMENTARY

Dialogue such as that in *The Day They Shot John Lennon*, and *Educating Rita* may be described as naturalistic, reflecting real social situations. In Oscar Wilde's dialogue however, and that of *The Big Sleep*, there is a distinct element of stylisation in the writing.

Stylisation occurs when a writer exaggerates a natural feature eg of conversation or behaviour so that it becomes very noticeable and is taken as typical. Handled well, the language used shifts the everyday into a perspective that is intriguing, amusing, or perhaps, horrifying. Dickens' writing is stylised in the *Our Mutual Friend* excerpts. It creates foreboding and also grotesque comedy. Chandler's writing is stylised too; it creates a tough, hard-boiled attitude that became the name of a whole genre of American detective stories. The 'style' is picked up in the film noir genre as demonstrated in the screenplay: dialogue with attitude, you might call it.

## *The Last To Go by Harold Pinter*

### ACTIVITY 51

The next drama text you are going to examine is in fact a full length sketch for radio by a master stylist, Harold Pinter. Read *The Last to Go* aloud with a partner. After a first run through, think about how important the pauses and the timing will be in performance.

Identify the elements of everyday conversation that have been 'stylised'. In themselves they may seem very ordinary but explain the overall effect of this kind of dramatic writing. Do you agree that the sketch can seem comic from one perspective and bleakly tragic from another? How can this be so?

A coffee stall A BARMAN and an old NEWSPAPER SELLER. The BARMAN leans on his counter. The OLD MAN stands with tea. Silence.

| | |
|---|---|
| MAN | You was a bit busier earlier. |
| BARMAN | Ah. |
| MAN | Round about ten. |
| BARMAN | Ten. was it? |
| MAN | About then. |
| | *Pause.* |
| MAN | I passed by here about then. |
| BARMAN | Oh yes? |
| MAN | I noticed you were doing a bit of trade. |
| | *Pause.* |
| BARMAN | Yes, trade was very brisk here about ten. |
| MAN | Yes. I noticed. |
| | *Pause.* |
| | I sold my last one about then. Yes. About nine forty-five. |
| BARMAN | Sold your last then, did you? |
| MAN | Yes, my last 'Evening News' it was. Went about twenty to ten. |
| | Pause. |
| BARMAN | 'Evening News', was it? |
| MAN | Yes. |
| | *Pause.* |
| | Sometimes it's the 'Star' is the last to go. |
| BARMAN | Ah. |
| MAN | Or the . . . whatsisname. |
| BARMAN | 'Standard'. |
| MAN | Yes. |
| | *Pause.* |

All I had left tonight was the 'Evening News'.
*Pause.*

BARMAN Then that went, did it?
MAN Yes.
*Pause.*
Like a shot.
*Pause.*
BARMAN You didn't have any left, eh?
MAN No. Not after I sold that one.
*Pause.*
BARMAN It was after that you must have come by here then, was it?
MAN Yes. I come by here after that, see, after I packed up.
BARMAN You didn't stop here though, did you?
MAN When?
BARMAN I mean, you didn't stop here and have a cup of tea then, did you?
MAN What, about ten?
BARMAN Yes.
MAN No, I went up to Victoria.
BARMAN No, I thought I didn't see you.
MAN I had to go up to Victoria.
*Pause.*
BARMAN Yes, trade was very brisk here about then.
*Pause.*
MAN I went to see if I could get hold of George.
BARMAN Who?
MAN George.
*Pause.*
BARMAN George who?
MAN George ... whatsisname.
BARMAN Oh.
Did you get hold of him?
MAN No. No. I couldn't get hold of him. I couldn't locate him.
BARMAN He's not much about now, is he?
*Pause.*
MAN When did you last see him then?
BARMAN Oh, I haven't seen him for years.
MAN No, nor me.
*Pause.*
BARMAN Used to suffer very bad from arthritis.
MAN Arthritis?
BARMAN Yes.
MAN He never suffered from arthritis.
BARMAN Suffered very bad.
*Pause.*
MAN Not when I knew him.
*Pause.*
BARMAN I think he must have left the area.
*Pause.*
MAN Yes, it was the 'Evening News' was the last to go tonight.
BARMAN Not always the last though, is it, though?
MAN No. Oh no. I mean sometimes it's the 'News'. Other times it's one of the others. No way of telling beforehand. Until you've got your last one left, of course. Then you can tell which one it's going to be.
BARMAN Yes.
Pause.
MAN Oh yes.
*Pause.*
I think he must have left the area.

# Summary

In this chapter you have explored the language of drama scripts, observing in particular relationships between conversation in 'real' life and scripted dialogue. You have also considered how performance conventions and expectations affect both the actors' delivery and the audience's response.

# 6 Literary Stylistics

## Survey

This final chapter is both a review of stylistics in relation to A-Level English Language syllabuses and an opportunity to revise what you have learned in this book. Activities are suggested at each stage.

The only difference between literary stylistics and any other kind of stylistics is that the texts explored will be narrative fiction, verse and drama written for the purposes of verbal art and entertainment. It is important however not to start from an evaluative position, treating literary texts and 'good writing' as synonymous. Good writing can be found in genres other than narrative fiction, verse and drama: autobiography, biography, history, travel writing, sports reporting, music criticism are just some examples in which good writing may be found. There is a zone, it would seem, where features of fictional writing such as imagination, sophistication, strong (or subtle) personal voice, merge with the characteristics of factual writing. It is also evident that many expected features of fictional narratives, poetry and drama are used very effectively in modern advertising: storylines, dialogue, language play, verse, figures of speech.

**ACTIVITY 52**

Collect three or four examples of 'factual' writing that impress you because they are well written and have 'literary' qualites.

Identify some of the things they have in common with 'fictional' writing.

## What is stylistics?

There's an old joke that usually provokes a groan: What ARE stylistics? Joking apart, it is certainly true that a useful way of viewing stylistics is to see it as a very plural kind of activity. It requires you in fact, to apply what you have learned from your syllabus as a whole to any spoken or written text you may be investigating: language and society and language varieties (always), language acquisition and language change (sometimes), phonology, grammar, lexis, semantics, pragmatics, discourse (all of these ways). By reading a text from these perspectives, a degree of objectivity can be brought to bear on the other essential and inevitable component of reading, namely your own subjectivity. Students in examinations show themselves very responsive to lexis; stylistics requires a reader to take that initial responsiveness further. John Haynes writes of this balancing of objectivity and subjectivity as follows: 'Studying style may be very much more than a fascination with words, but it is nothing without it'.

Here is one way of mind-mapping stylistics; it follows a particular sequence of syllabus content but it could begin at different starting points and follow other sequences. The important thing is to be able to apply all or most of the syllabus elements to any text.

# Varieties of writing

Readers have very little difficulty in identifying literary texts or verbal art. Fragments are sufficient:

- Three Blind Mice
- . . . she said, smiling to herself.
- Exit backstage right
- My heart aches . . .
- Now read on
- . . . gentle reader . . .
- There was a young lady from . . .

Genre clues such as these make it quite easy to reconstruct likely forms, vocabulary, register conventions and even the content in which such fragments would be embedded.

**ACTIVITY 53**

Take each of the above fragments and place it in a quite unexpected genre, where the fragment may be used for particular effect, for example, the plot of a thriller entitled *Three Blind Mice* or a satirical account of a political meeting described in stage management terms, *Exit the Independent Green candidate backstage right.*

Readers intuitively place texts in genres and it helps in stylistics to keep genre in mind. You need to recognise though, where features of different genre are mixed in a text and where there are inter-textual or cross-genre references.

In the above activity you were engaged in a kind of rule breaking, common in verbal art. Rule breaking is not necessarily a rebellious act; it is a means of creating novelty, surprise, interest and sometimes profundity, by not fulfilling conventions or expectations. In this sense, all art breaks the rules, to avoid the predictable and to create entertaining surprises. Jazz improvisations are often unpredictable, hence the description of jazz as 'the sound of surprise'.

## Phonology and speech

Novels, short stories, poems and drama scripts can be categorised in a variety of written genres and sub-genres but any literary text can also be described in terms of its speech elements. The style of one text may be utterly remote from everyday talk and yet another may seem very 'colloquial'. The fact that a novel contains dialogue is no guarantee that the dialogue will sound like 'real' conversation. Conversely, long narrative stretches in a story may sound very much like everyday, intimate, personal chat. You need to hear the voices coming through, and even the changes in voice that can occur in literary texts.

**ACTIVITY 54**

With a partner, collect three or four novels, and read aloud a section of dialogue. Ask yourselves how believable it is as real talk. Bear in mind that it may not be a kind of talk you hear everyday. The central question is: Do people really talk like this?

Three questions follow from this:

1 Is the talk unconvincing or stereotypical?
2 Is the talk extremely natural or 'realistic'?
3 Is the talk stylised? This means: does the talk follow conventions that readers would expect in a novel – close to real life but shaped for an imagined context; realistic enough yet capable of interesting a reader who is 'outside' it. It may be very stylised, as in the Dickens, Hardy, Wilde and Chandler excerpts.

Next, read to each other a narrative passage from the novel and listen for the voice of the storyteller. Imagine what kind of a 'face' is speaking; catch the right tone in the voice. How does it contrast with the characters' voices?

You can carry out this activity with two or three playscripts, asking the same three questions. The final issue about narrative voice is not directly relevant, though if you are looking at a play by someone like George Bernard Shaw, where you will find an authorial voice in his detailed, often lengthy, stage directions.

**ACTIVITY 55**

Drawing on examples in this book, identify instances where literary talk can be close to everyday life, and where it can seem very remote. Note that the term, 'real life' has not been used here because the artistic achievement of writers such as Shakespeare, Donne, Dickens, Hardy, Wilde gives their creations as much reality in readers' minds as the day-to-day events of their lives.

If literature is stylised writing, even when it appears very 'natural', poetry can be regarded as exceptionally stylised writing. It draws on the metrical and phonological resources of language and by foregrounding, emphasises, even exaggerates, features of natural speech to achieve nuances of meaning beyond literal word and sentence meanings. The term 'affective' best describes the way in which these additional meanings are communicated. In the 18th century, critics held the notion that 'instruction' could be achieved by 'giving delight'. If we take instruction to mean 'teaching' or reflecting on life and love, for example, the delight conveyed by metre and word sounds are not just a bonus but an integral part of the 'lesson'. The very art and craft required to construct a poem like Donne's *Holy Sonnet* is as much an act of defiance against death as anything the poem actually says.

**ACTIVITY 56**

Taking examples from this book, identify and explain one or two ways in which poetry draws on the sounds and rhythms of everyday English and transforms them.

# Lexis and grammar

Frequently, linguists use the term 'lexico-grammatical' to describe stylistic effects. It is a very sensible recognition that in matters of style the two are inseparable, given that words are the raw material of grammatical structures. 'Doing things with words' is also a useful notion of grammar in action. Often, too, meanings (semantics) are best explained by reference to both the dictionary meaning of the lexis and its particular grammatical use in a text. A-Level examiners are looking for ways in which candidates show their understanding of the interdependence of words and grammar in the construction of meaning. To do this you need to see lexis, grammar and meaning as a closely related trio. For tidy revision purposes, they are listed separately in the following pages but the activities keep them related. It is rather like practising your backhand volley but knowing you will only use it along with forehand strokes and serves in the context of a real tennis game.

## *Lexis*

All the words used in a text should be viewed as choices, made consciously or unconsciously. Indeed, as already observed, many words choose themselves. In verbal art, a good deal of editorial thinking (monitoring, quality control, censoring) is required to achieve the 'right' effect. If it 'just comes' you are lucky; often it is a case of what T. S. Eliot described as 'the intolerable wrestle with words'. If the chosen words are very effective, as in the examples in this book, it is difficult to know what to say about them. One way forward is to recognise that English is a language extraordinarily rich in synonyms. Giving consideration to alternatives that might have been used usually shows up the distinctive nuance of meaning in the one actually chosen. Context too, of course, adds meaning.

## ACTIVITY 57

Look at the following synonyms:

- thinking
- reasoning
- rational
- cerebral
- intellectual.

They can all be used as adjectives to describe a person, each conveying a different nuance of meaning. (Which one would you apply to Bradley Headstone, for example?).

Write a sentence or two describing someone and using one of the above words. Now replace your choice with each of the others in turn, and decide which you prefer. Put in writing what you think the nuance of meaning is.

Next, rewrite the sentence but this time change the grammar by using each of these synonyms as a noun:

- thought
- reason
- rationality
- cerebrum
- intellect.

You will need to find appropriate new phrases too. For example, 'a thinking man' might become, 'a man who gave much thought to things'.

1 What differences do you detect in tone (an element of style)?
2 Which do you prefer, adjectives or nouns? Or does your preference vary?

Now try the following pairs, noticing how you have to change the structure (ie word sequences), even bringing in new words, as you shift from adjectival to noun uses:

Note that 'harm', 'damage' and 'hurt' can also be used as verbs. When you have used them as nouns, rewrite your original sentences to incorporate the use of these words as verbs. Again, notice the stylistic twists and turns necessary to do this.

It is not long before observations on lexis turn into observations on grammar.

| | |
|---|---|
| harmful | harm |
| injurious | injury |
| damaging | damage |
| detrimental | detriment |
| hurtful | hurt |

Observations on lexis that contribute to a fuller understanding of meanings are:

- recurring prefixes, other prefixes and negative forms
- patterns of antonyms and synonyms
- sequences of adjectives and adjective/noun pairs
- rule breaking words ('slang', taboo words, euphemisms)
- jargon words
- abstractions and concrete words
- etymological origins, for example Latinate words.

## Grammar

It is useful and not particularly difficult to identify dynamic and stative verbs, or relatively dynamic or stative verbs. Often taken for granted however, are uses of the auxiliaries 'to be' and 'to have' which, since they signify existence and possession are important in their own right. Consider:

- I think, therefore I am.
- I am the state (L'etat c'est moi).
- In the beginning was the word.
- God is love.
- I am the way.
- This is it!
- We have lift-off.
- You are a has-been.
- I am a wannabe.

All these require interpretation to lose their enigmatic quality. Other forms appear more straightforward:

- 'is happy'
- 'am sad'
- 'will be successful'
- 'was the best'.

The verb is followed by an adjective in each case. Sometimes the verb is followed by an adverb, as in 'I was there'. A succession of such verb forms plus adjective denoting a state creates a particular stylistic effect in a text, stative rather than dynamic. Don't confuse 'stative' with 'static' in the sense of 'stationary'. Stative sequences contrast with dynamic sequences in that the latter convey a more immediate sense of action.

The verb 'to have' is also taken for granted, yet it denotes possession and in its use expresses a separation between person and thing: 'has a problem' 'had an operation' 'will have a BMW one day'.

Note the difference not only in register choice but also in verb choice in the following:

- They have a lot of attitude.
- They are awkward buggers.

Parallelism and balancing effects, reversals and any deviations from conventional word order are immediately noticeable. Our minds are full of syntactic patterns, thousands of memory traces, into which we expect words to fit. In verbal art, the language draws attention to itself in some way; it foregrounds something the writer wishes to draw particular attention to.

Here are some first lines of poems for example which begin with the word 'that'. Compare their use of the word.

'That's my last duchess painted on the wall'

Browning, *My Last Duchess*

'That time of year thou mayst in me behold'

Shakespeare, *Sonnet 73*

That Whitsun, I was late getting away'

Larkin, *The Whitsun Weddings*

'That night your great guns, unawares'

Hardy, *Channel Firing*

'That is no country for old men.'

Yeats, *Sailing To Byzantium*

'That which her slender waist confined'

Waller, *On A Girdle*

'That night the whole world mingled'

Chesterton, *A Certain Evening*

'That she is beautiful is not delight'

Augusta Webster, *Mother and Daughter Sonnet Sequence*

'That some day Death who has us all for jest Shall hide me in the dark and voiceless mould'

Webster, *ibid*

'That poets are far rarer births than kings Your noblest father proved.'

Jonson, *To Elizabeth, Countess of Rutland, the daughter of Sir Philip Sidney.*

## ACTIVITY 58

Collect other examples of poetic ideas, foregrounded by a grammatical feature, for example:

'To err is human: to forgive divine.'

Pope

'It is a far, far better thing that I do, than I have ever done; it is a far, far better rest that I go to, than I have ever known.'

Dickens, *A Tale of Two Cities*

Two aspects of language and life that are brought together by grammar are time and place. The tense system enables verbs to signal time precisely, while prepositions and adverbs signal the location of nouns and where verbs took place. These are features of language present in all texts and are therefore part of the repertoire of literary stylistics. Their effects are just as specific and just as pervasive as recurring uses of 'to be' and 'to have'. Note, for example in *Ozymandias* that the first two verbs are in the past tense (I met, who said). The traveller's story uses the present tense (stand, lies, tell) yet verbs relating to the sculptor are in the past tense. The time scale of the poem seems to stretch back to boundless space and eternal time, the last verb, 'stretch' in an eternal present tense. Features such as these are worth noting because in the imagination of both readers and writers, time and space can be mapped out in very different ways from real, chronological time.

Always keep an eye open for grammatical words that signal time (when, then, after, before) and location (there, where, within, beyond). The trick is not to make heavy weather of them, in an examination answer for example, but always to be aware of them in case they offer you a useful line of thought or enquiry.

With sentence length (countable) and structure (shape), avoid describing examples as 'very complex' or 'complicated'. If you mean 'difficult to read', say so, and look more closely at the elements in the sentence. Assuming the sentence isn't syntactically flawed, not at all likely in an examination, look for such things as:

- lexical density (lots of nouns, abstract noun phrases, unusual adjectives, more than two main verbs)
- sentence rhythm (if you get this wrong, whether in prose or poetry, you are likely to misread the meaning)
- the function being performed by the sentence (for example, the sudden appearance of an imperative)
- the role of a sentence in relation to preceding and succeeding sentences.

The last point is in effect, about continuity or cohesion. As a rule of thumb you could spot an important aspect of cohesion by plotting through a text the first word or two after every full stop.

# Semantics

Take two contemporary novels, *Hi Fidelity* by Nick Hornby and *Trainspotting* by Irvine Welsh and think how they would have been received by readers in the 1890s. We can guess at what would be incomprehensible and at what would have occasioned public outbursts of distaste and shock. We cannot however be entirely sure at private responses. Think also about how readers may regard these books in the 2090s. We cannot even be sure that they will even be in print or remembered.

Literary works are products of their age though the genre to which they belong is likely to be older and likely to continue from one generation to another. Successive generations of readers extend the life of a novel or a poem, while generations of theatre companies and theatregoers keep plays alive. But interpretations change over the years, just as a changing society creates new kinds of readers. It should not be surprising that A-Level English Literature candidates, taking an examination in 1995, the 50th anniversary year of D-Day, much celebrated in all the media, brought that event to their interpretation of Matthew Arnold's poem, *Dover Beach,* written in 1867. The last line about 'ignorant armies clashing by night' is a timeless line.

Many meanings can be shared with departed generations, but new meanings may be added too. Semantic issues that you need to be aware of when reading literary texts of any age are:

- your own role and entitlement as a meaning maker
- the possibility of other interpretations or 'readings'
- the presence of unstated, implied, meanings in texts
- ways of resolving apparent obscurity (Is the writer saying something that is inherently difficult? Or are you reading something into the text)
- the use of metaphor (Are they over familiar ones? Startlingly original? Obscure?)

- features of the text take on, or look like they might take on, symbolic meaning? (This is not the same as metaphor. Consider the symbolic content of *Ozymandias* for example.)
- any ambiguities in the text that add dimensions of contrasted meaning?
- historical linguistic features that need to be taken into account (Changes in word meaning? Syntax? The words themselves?)

# Discourse

It is important to keep clear in your mind a distinction between fiction, fact and reality. Fiction and fact are normally opposites but both are a part of reality. Novels and poems have a real existence in the imagination once you have read and experienced them. The emotions and impressions they generate in readers and the thoughts they provoke are all real in the mind of the reader. The language itself is real, shared cultural property and as such, offers a writer opportunities for original expression within accumulated rules and conventions. These rules, conventions and expectations make up what is known as discourse.

A useful contribution to understanding literary texts as a variety of discourse is provided by text grammarians such as Halliday and Hasan in *Language, Context and Text* (1985) and also in Hasan's *Linguistics, Language and Verbal Art* (1989). In their view, cohesion is the surface continuity of the text while coherence is a deeper continuity. Leech and Short take a similar view in *Style in Fiction* (1981), emphasising an interpersonal element in reading and writing in which meanings are constructed in the text and in the context of a particular genre. This is how literary communication works, the text acting as a meeting place for writers and readers. You could regard discourse, so far as stylistics is concerned, as a two way process of tuning into the right wavelength.

It helps to think of discourse as a verb rather than a noun. To discourse is to start off a communication, to run it on and to stop when you have said what you want to say in an appropriate way. Within the running on (the original Latin word 'discurrere' means 'to run about') there will be all kinds of twists and turns, strategies and variations, before reaching a satisfactory conclusion. Overall framing of content is also very important.

'Discourse' as a noun refers to the products of this process. Non-literary (that is, not verbal art) forms are history, geography, medicine, law, the physical sciences, statistics and business management. Examples of literary discourse (verbal art) have been explored in this book. In literary discourse, writers follow conventions that readers expect but there is also room for flouting those conventions and for breaking rules.

If the whole of the language is imagined as a house, then discourses are different uses of that language confined to particular rooms in which everybody knows what the rules are. A stranger in any room may be lost to begin with, while the expert will have to make considerable discourse adjustment if he is to explain what goes on in his room to people in another room altogether, for example, statisticians talking to poets or medical researchers to a popular newspaper. The stylistician, incidentally, is the one wandering about the house observing the different ways in which different interest groups use a common language to create such a variety of meanings. In the process of these wanderings, differences of status and power between discourses become noticeable. Some discourses have acquired more power in our lives than others.

## ACTIVITY 59

Look at *Miss Brill* and ask yourself, what kind of discourse is this? Who is talking to whom?

Write three or four maxims for storytelling, basing them on what seems essential in the story. Then test them out on other stories you know to see if they conform to your maxims.

The critic John Berger suggests two maxims for storytelling are 'scepticism' and 'compassion' (Granta, No. 21, 1987). You don't have to include these; they are just examples. Remember though, that your prime concern is to be able to identify, describe and explain your maxims in specific features of language used. How much 'scepticism' or 'compassion' do you detect in Miss Brill, for example?

You could do the same with poetry. Look at any poem in this book; write three or four maxims for poetry and then see if other poems conform.

In the broadest sense, literary discourse (verbal art) is how storytellers and poets address readers and this mode of address is realised in specific texts within a genre. The text 'runs on' as it were, and when you do a running commentary you are running with it. Other metaphors in modern literary communication theory are 'going with the grain' (deconstruction is deliberately reading against the grain); unpacking the implied meanings 'the implicatures); tuning-in to the wavelength; following the woven threads (cohesion in discourse). Cohesion in a novel is the linkage and consistency of time, place and relations; coherence is achieved by theme and plot.

## ACTIVITY 60

A key aspect of cohesion that often gives a strong clue to the type of discourse is the first word after every full stop. Look at any prose excerpt in this book and note down the sequence of initial words in each sentence. How does each word connect its sentence to, or follow from, the preceding sentence?

## ACTIVITY 61

Read your chosen excerpt again, and plot its coherence. You can do this by noting the ways in which your attention is shifted by new things (often nouns and noun phrases, concrete or abstract) introduced by the writer. Put on one side your own subjective trains of thought, for the moment, and concentrate on the linguistic evidence, that is the writer's own choice of nouns and verbs.

Do not be confused by alternative terminology or variations in the idea of discourse. The word is, after all, a metaphor, as its origin shows. It describes usefully but not very systematically, varieties of spoken and written language. In the previous activities you concentrated on prose fiction and poems. You also need to look at drama excerpts in this book and explore whether there are discourse differences introduced by the practical circumstances of playscripts for large audiences.

The term 'discourse' is not unconnected with 'register' which describes the distinctive voice or manner of address in a text. 'Address' and 'voice' are key concepts. In a novel, for example, dialogue is a discourse embedded within the discourse of the novel as a whole. Admittedly, the novel as a whole will 'frame' any dialogue but we nevertheless expect from a half-decent novelist, dialogue that has some life of its own.

Discourse within discourse is especially noticeable in novels featuring dialect conversations. The discourse of Wegg and Venus is different from that of Charlie Hexam and Bradley Headstone. In *Ozymandias*, there is a discussion between the 'I' and the reader; within that there is the discussion between the traveller and the 'I'; within that there is the imperative discourse of Ozymandias himself to the rest of the world.

In the narrative too there can be varieties of discourse used for effect. At the end of the Silas Wegg excerpt, for example, Dickens deliberately uses the discourse of scientific classification in which specimens are itemised and classified. Note the placing of adjectives after nouns to maintain strict alphabetical ordering. This is yet another example of 'intertextuality', which can be defined as the echoing of one kind of text in another.

Sometimes 'discourse' and 'text' seem to be used interchangeably but it is tidier to think of discourse as the repertoire of conventions and resources for particular kinds of writing or speaking, and texts as specific realisations in time and place.

In the work of the French critic, Michel Foucault, discourse is seen as a transmitter of ideologies. By this he means that values and beliefs about life and the world (anything and everything, more or less) are embedded in the way we write about things, especially in advertising, politics, poetry, fiction and journalism. For Foucault, different discourses between teacher and student, psychoanalyst and patient, lawyer and client are practices in which students, patients and clients are persuaded to see themselves and the world in particular ways. The idea of discourse as an activity or social practice is also central to the work of Norman Fairclough though his concerns are not with verbal art. Literature could be regarded as cultural practice.

One remark of Foucault's is worth bearing in mind when thinking about literary texts:

> In my books I do like to make fictional use of the materials I assemble or put together, and I deliberately make fictional constructions with authentic elements.

'Fictional constructions with authentic elements' could be a definition of verbal art.

**ACTIVITY 62**

Compare any two poems or prose excerpts in this book and decide if an ideology is being transmitted in the writing. Remember, you are looking for implicit values and beliefs which you may or may not share. The idea of a text as a meeting place for readers and writers communicating implicit as well as explicit meanings takes us into the field of pragmatics.

# Pragmatics

Pragmatics, as linguists know it today, began as the study of how speakers and listeners understand implied and contextual meanings during conversation. Words cannot be taken at face (or 'ear') value; some agendas are hidden; texts have subtexts which are only accessible to inference. There is a general concern about mis-communication and the potential everywhere for misreading. It is evident in popular expressions: Do you get my meaning?; What I mean to say is...; Do you see what I mean?

The term 'literary pragmatics' has now come into use, referring to interpersonal signals, connections, shared meanings, between a writer and a reader. A writer's tone for example may be alienating because it is interpreted as inflexible, arrogant, supercilious, unsympathetic, cold or clinical. Something very simple such as the unexpected use of the modal verb 'might', as in the beginning of one of the Fleming excerpts, immediately elicits curiosity in a reader. It may of course irritate other readers. In *Miss Brill* there are many nuances of tone that affect the reader's response and direct what D. H. Lawrence called 'the ebb and flow of sympathy' in the reader. The reader has acquired an important role in modern criticism as an accomplice of the writer in the process of making meanings. As long ago as 1831, however, the poet Coleridge wrote that readers needed a faith that a poem had something valuable to offer and that a 'willing suspension of disbelief' was necessary for that poetic faith. This could of course be a way of saying 'go with the ideological flow' (see Foucault). Modern stylistics requires you to be both an acquiescent reader and a critical one too.

The art of storytelling, of getting a reader/listener's attention depends to a large extent on what William Labov calls the 'tellability' of the tale. In *Language in the Inner City* he considers tellability in oral narratives, looking at how interest is aroused and maintained by a 'good story'. Others have applied the idea to written narratives.

**ACTIVITY 63**

Draw up a list of features that make 'a good story' from the reader/listener's point of view. You may include the journalistic sense of a good story as well as the fictional sense. You may find it easier to consider listening and reading as separate cases.

What 'makes' a story 'tellable'?

Actors and stand-up comics all express their gratitude for a good audience. What makes a 'good' live audience? What makes a 'good' reader compared to a 'good' audience?

The notion of performance is directly applicable to stories and poems in public readings, and it transfers to the experience of reading as you become more familiar with the personality or the style of the writer. It is also applicable to film and TV.

With plays performed live in the theatre, performance has a very distinct meaning and relevance. Live audiences interact in very real ways with the actors on the stage. Features not immediately or at all discernible in the written text such as timing, humour, emotional intensity, pace and physical presence have to be supplied or realised by actors according to performing conventions. These have palpable effects on real audiences.

When analysing playscripts, or dialogue in a novel, it is important not to mistake the pragmatics of verbal art for the pragmatics of real life. You certainly would not do this in the theatre because of the recognised element of 'performance'. Dramatists draw on their knowledge and understanding of what goes on in real conversation (implied meanings; power play; misunderstandings; silences) to develop character through dialogue but, as with everything else pragmatic, experience in life is transformed into verbal art on the page and on the stage.

**ACTIVITY 64**

Look at the excerpt from *Educating Rita* and compare it with *The Importance of Being Earnest.* Identify one or two ways in which people handle conversations in real life, and which have been re-constructed into theatre. What is the art that lies behind the dialogue?

Radio listeners have observed that when they switch on, they always know, even after a second or so, whether they are listening to speech in a play or to real speech in, say, an interview or a radio talk.

Try this out yourself. You could even record very brief snatches of radio talk of different kinds and sequence them on audio tape. Ask other students to identify scripted drama and explain how they knew.

# Language acquisition

It may seem a sudden turn from discourse to language acquisition, yet there is a strong connection if you remember that language acquisition is a life-long process. Acquiring the ability to read different kinds of books is an essential element in education. Getting on different wavelengths, evaluating critically and reading inferences all have to be learned. A poet's style, for example, may take a bit of getting used to before it begins to 'speak' to a reader. It's also true that readers 'go off' the style of a novelist because it is at odds with their present frame of mind, only to return in later years with a new enthusiasm. Remember Roland Barthes' notion of 'writerly' texts – texts that do not immediately yield enjoyment or understanding.

**ACTIVITY 65**

Make an inventory of the literary characters, stories and quotations (even half remembered ones) that have stuck in your mind. The truth is that there will be many more than you can record, but it will be interesting to see which ones you actually recollect: nursery rhymes, fairy stories, classic tales. If you wish to consider film and TV as well, make a separate list since one aspect of reading, namely imagining, is not quite the same in visual media as in print media.

Try also to recollect novels, plays and poems that you have not been able to 'get into'. Look at one example again and identify just what it is that puts you off. It is useful in stylistics to be aware of your own negative responses; sometimes it may be due to a blind spot, at other times you may be completely justified in your rejection of a text.

From a sociological point of view, everyday language is a prime socialising agent in a child's life, teaching not only words but the values and ideologies encoded in those words. This is what structuralism is all about; the ways in which language names the structures in which we live: family relationships, pecking orders, economic necessities, moral beliefs, sexual practices and taboos. Once named they become internalised and lived out in the mind as well as in life.

From the psychological point of view, verbal art is a prime agent in children's imaginative development, filling their minds with myths, legends, heroes, wise sayings, fables, and all kinds of plot structures and word rituals from 'Once upon a time . . .' to '. . . but it was all a dream'. In early childhood, fact and fiction have the same reality and children gradually learn to dissociate the two. In adult life, fact and fiction have different realities. You need only consider the nation's insatiable appetite for soap operas on TV and the considerable popularity of science fiction to see the continuing importance of fictions in adult life.

**ACTIVITY 66**

Look at an example of science fiction or of a multi-volume fantasy tale by Tolkien, Donaldson or Robert Jordan, for example. You could also look at Terry Pratchett.
How far do you think such books are accurately described as 'escapism' and how far are they something else? To answer these questions you will need to explore just what linguistic effects the writer is using.

1 What kind of language have the writer and reader acquired?
2 What kind of imagining do they share?
3 Do you detect any evidence of language change in the lexical content and the style of writing?

# Language change

Nowhere is language change more evident than in English Literature. Any selection of excerpts from the Old English *Beowulf*, through Middle English Malory and Chaucer, on to the Early Modern English of Shakespeare and through to modern times will demonstrate changes in phonology, lexis, grammar, semantics and style. Yet a great many generic features remain, creating a tradition that allows for variations on a theme.

**ACTIVITY 67**

Take the theme (loneliness?) and the sequence of events in *Miss Brill* and rewrite the story in what you would regard as a literary style for the 1990s. Alternatively, modernise the excerpt from *The Importance of Being Earnest*.
Pay particular attention to all the contextual changes of social attitudes and language style that have occurred. Remember though that your writing will need to be as carefully crafted as Mansfield's or Wilde's, to catch the nuances of your own times as they caught the nuances of theirs.

# Language and society

Having looked in this overview at language varieties, phonology and speech, lexis, grammar, semantics, discourse, pragmatics, language acquisition and language change, we finally arrive at the most enveloping syllabus area of all, language and society, the place where stylistics begins and ends.

Stylistic analysis of literary texts isn't just the dissection of language to find out how a text is constructed, it is a way of reading how the content of the text has been imagined. Novels, poems and plays are powerful mixtures of language, life and imagination. By focusing attention on the language, stylistic leads to greater understanding and enjoyment of how writers transform elements from life into imagined experience that can be shared and reconstructed by readers. Verbal art depends on both imagination and language.

# Bibliography

## Research reading

The following books are recommended because they demonstrate a variety of linguistic approaches to verbal art. Don't think of them as books you are obliged to read from cover to cover; they are workbooks and you should select a section that interests you and go through it in detail.

**1** *Studying Literature: Theory and Practice for Senior Students* by Brian Moon (1990). An Australian book published in the UK by The English and Media Centre, 136, Chalton Street, London NW1 1RX.
Look, for example, at the section on Dickens' *Hard Times*, and compare it with the approach here to *Our Mutual Friend*. There is also a good section on reading and gender which includes an exploration of a poem by John Donne.

**2** *Introducing Stylistics* by John Haynes (1989), Unwin Hyman.
In Part Two (p 212) there is an exploration of Angela Carter's *The Snow Child*. Compare this with the exploration here of *Miss Brill*. You could also compare it with Moon's exploration of her story, *The Company of Wolves*. Look also at the section on Bessie Smith's recording of *Empty Bed Blues* (p 197).

**3** *Exploring Pre-Twentieth Century Fiction* by Angela Goddard (1995), Framework Press.
This is a large ring binder of photocopiable material intended mainly for GCSE courses. Don't, however, be put off by that. The author applies a wide range of linguistic ideas and methods to a very wide range of English Literature texts. If you didn't encounter this book in your own O-Level/GCSE course, now is your chance.

**4** *The Language of Fiction* by Keith Sanger (1998), Routledge.
Look at the two sections on Constructing Character, which consider the uses of description and dialogue. The final chapter gives yet another answer to the question, 'What is Literature?'.

**5** *Seeing Through Language* by Ron Carter and Walter Nash (1990), Blackwell.
Look, for example, at the section comparing Anita Bookner's description of a hotel (Hotel du Lac) with two advertisements for hotels. Behind this

comparison lies the idea of a 'cline' of writing ranging from the verbal art of poems and novels to mundane advertisements in tourist handbooks. At all points between lie fascinating mixtures of verbal art and everyday stuff.

**6** *The Language of Poetry* by John Macrae (1998), Routledge.
You could start by comparing McRae's exploration of Shelley's *Ozymandias* (p 35) with the one here. Look also at Unit Two on the sounds of poetry.

7 *Style* by John Haynes (1995), Routledge.
A short book not specifically concerned with literary texts (verbal art) but there are two very relevant and interesting sections. In 'Selection of Significant Detail', Haynes explores different versions of the story, *Pinocchio* (pp 49–53). The full texts are in an appendix. Pages 63–67 look at what the author calls 'verbal miming' in poetry.

**8** *Ways of Reading* by Martin Montgomery, Alan Dunant, Nigel Fabb, Tom Furniss and Sara Mills (1992), Routledge.
Gives the notion of 'reading' a much wider and more exciting meaning than merely decoding print on the page. It includes film narrative techniques and the 'language' of cinema. Look at the section on juxtaposition.

**9** *Language Play* by David Crystal (1998), Penguin. A book that shows how language play is central to our lives and every bit as important in language for conveying information. Pages 93–148 consider in turn headline writers, advertisers, comedians, poets, novelists and playwrights.

# Reference Books

*A Dictionary of Stylistics* by Katie Wales (1989), Longman.
Very comprehensive and authoritative. It is clearly written but be prepared to work at some of the definitions. It is neither your fault, nor the author's; some of them are very difficult but nonetheless interesting.

*Language and Literature: An Introductory Reader in Stylistics* ed by Ron Carter (1982), Allen and Unwin.
This is still a useful collection illustrating major issues and different approaches to language and literature.

*Linguistics and Literature* by Nigel Fabb (1997), Routledge.
Explains and illustrates the idea of verbal art. Its scope is global and makes the reader look at traditional English Literature texts in a wider cultural as well as linguistic context.

*Re-reading Literature* by Sue Hackman and Barbara Marshall (1990), Hodder and Stoughton.
Another book that widens the context to include gender issues and cultural changes that have affected our ideas of literature, non-print media and verbal art.